Sri Sathya Sai Baba

Sai Baba's Mahavakya* on LEADERSHIP

Book for Youth, Parents and Teachers

by
Padma Bhushan
Lt. Gen. (Ret.) Dr. M. L. Chibber
PVSM, AVSM, Ph.D.

*Mahavakya is a Sanskrit word meaning a great saying. The word is used for divine aphorisms in the ancient Indian scriptures, like "that thou art," which convey the eternal truth.

LEELA PRESS INC.
A Non-Profit Corporation
Faber, VA

Published by:
LEELA PRESS INC.
Rt. 1, Box 339C
Faber, VA 22938
(804) 361-1130

Originally published by
M & M International Publishers
Care, Grindlays Bank
10 E. Connaught Place
New Delhi-110 001, India
©1994, Sai Veera

Library of Congress Catalog No. 95-077760
Sai Baba's Mahavakya on Leadership

ISBN 0-9629835-4-3

Typeset in 11 point Times Roman
Printed in the United States by McNaughton & Gunn, Inc.

DEDICATED
with love and gratitude
to
Sri Sathya Sai Baba

I want you to be leaders to protect the world.
Leaders like lions____self-reliant, courageous,
majestic and just. The lion is the king of animals,
and I want you to be king among men.

Sai Baba
Inaugural Address to Students
Sri Sathya Sai Institute of Higher Learning
Summer Course, 1992

Bhagavan Sri Sathya Sai Baba

FOREWORD

LEADERSHIP IS IDEALISM IN ACTION

Man can discharge the tasks he takes up properly only when he understands the true significance of humanness.

It should be realised that the body, the mind and the Atma (the Self) together constitute the human being. The first (body) concerns action. The second (mind) relates to cognition. The third relates to Being. Action, Cognition and Being together make up humanness.

In this world, whatever a man wants to achieve, the first requisite is the body. Anything can be accomplished only through the body. The body is therefore identified with action. And then, to determine what is good or bad, right or wrong, true or false, sinful or meritorious, the power of enquiry and discrimination is used. This discriminating capacity resides in the mind. The mind is the instrument of cognition. Next, there is the Atmic Principle which is not subject to change and is firmly established in its Truth.

The unified expression of these three—body, mind and Atma—is called Sath-Chith-Ananda. "Sath" is that which Is. The principle which enables one to comprehend the physical, the mundane, the supramundane, and the scientific, is called "Chith". When "Sath" and "Chith" come together, there is "Ananda" (bliss). This is what a human being experiences through the body. Man is a manifestation of Sath-Chith-Ananda.

If, instead of experiencing this unity, man is concerned only about the body, he descends to the animal state. Animality is the state in which the body is not associated with the mind or the Atma. When the mind is not bound to the Atma or has no comprehension of its relation to the Atma, it turns demonic by its subjection to the body.

The Atma always remains divine, without any association with the body or the mind. But the total human personality becomes manifest only when there is harmonious unity between body, mind and the Atma.

If any individual is asked what he desires most, he will say "I wish to live long comfortably". But if people are asked further what they mean by comfort (sukham), most persons will have no clear answer. Many imagine that they must acquire wealth and enjoy all kinds of comforts to be happy. But true happiness does not consist in these. Happiness is also equated with living as one likes—"Svechcha",—moving about freely, doing as one pleases and spending one's time in feasting. This is not real "Svechcha". The term "Svechcha" consists of two words: Svaa + Ichcha. "Svaa" represents the Atmic principle "Ichcha" means "wish" or "desire". Real freedom implies reverence for the Self (Atma) and experiencing the bliss of the Self. One who has no faith in the Self allows egoistic conceit (Ahamkara) to grow and courts ruin. Conceit is the root of all evil.

Adherence to Truth, control of the senses, equanimity (santhi), forbearance and compassion are like five life-breaths for man. If these five life-sustaining qualities are to sanctify man's life, it is essential to maintain purity in thought, word and deed ("Trikarana Suddhi"). In addition, one aspiring to be a leader has to possess three types of knowledge: First; self-knowledge (that is, knowledge of his strengths and weaknesses). Two; knowledge relating to his field of work. Three; knowledge of the social environment. A good leader has to possess what may be called individual (or personal) character and national character. Only such persons can become ideal leaders. Giving up selfish interests, eschewing totally ideas of "mine" and "thine", the true leader should be dedicated to the welfare of all and uphold the reputation of his country. On all occasions he should march in front rather than issue orders from the rear. He should set the example by his actions. The world needs today leaders who will be guides in action.

Only the person who practises Sathya, Dharma, Santhi, Prema and Ahimsa (Truth, Righteousness, Peace, Love and Non-Violence), experiences joy therefrom and shares that joy with others, can be called a leader. In addition to these qualities, a good leader should be selfless and be imbued with the spirit of sacrifice (Thyaga). He should have only the people's welfare at heart and seek to win their approbation by his service. He must be prepared even to make the supreme sacrifice for the sake of the people. A leader is one who gives up all ideas of possessiveness, strives only for the well-being of society and holds himself forth as an ideal human being.

December 1993

Contents

Preface

The Sri Sathya Sai Institute of Higher Learning is probably the only university in the world that has a mandatory full-credit course on leadership for students in the master of business administration program. The Chancellor of the university, Sathya Sai Baba, had this course included in the curriculum for good and valid reasons.

In his mission to bring about the unity of man, which will consolidate the global economy and eventually lead to what Arnold Toynbee, the famous historian, calls a global state, good leadership will play a critical role. Another reason for the course is the confusion and grey areas that prevail in the modern world about this ancient human capability. We have gotten deeply obsessed with the primacy of "self-interest," with the result that the real foundation of leadership has become completely obscured. The universal experience in the history of mankind is that no one can really be a good leader without rising above self-interest. Yet in the "quick fix" and "made easy" recipes, theories and concepts about leadership developed and merrily marketed in this century, this fundamental truth has been completely sidetracked. The time has come to relearn the cardinal lesson that practice of human values (call them moral values if you wish) alone can nurture effective leaders.

Most of what is included in this book for youth, parents and teachers is the result of conceptual clarity provided by the Chancellor during years of research and experimentation; it is a synthesis of Eastern and Western experience of leadership. Indeed, much of the work was actually articulated by him during his frequent interaction with students and teachers involved in the leadership course.

The research related to this book was undertaken by the author from 1979 onwards. As commander of India's counteroffensive force, he was asked to examine if, with the forces allocated to him, he could not achieve better results than had been planned till then. Before finalizing the revised plans, he decided to get a feel for his commanders' views. After many weeks of visiting the formations and discussing the problems with them, he was left with a rather uncomfortable feeling.

The senior commanders and staff officers in his force felt that they could achieve much greater goals. However, they were unsure of the younger officers providing the requisite quality of leadership. When the author discreetly interacted with the younger officers, they left him with the feeling that they could achieve the impossible if only they had slightly better quality senior officers!

This dichotomy triggered off the research on how to improve leadership. This led to his undertaking a Ph.D. dissertation in a university, and after retiring from the army, becoming the chief executive of a management institute in India. The research has thus covered a very broad spectrum, and the quest still continues.

In 1990, the Chancellor of the Sai university approved converting the holistic and practical model that emerged from over a decade of research into a book for youth. At almost the same time, Indira Gandhi National Open University at New Delhi adopted the concept as a textbook for its M.B.A. students, who normally number around 5,000.

During the next two years, the model was presented to a cross section of students, young adults and adults, both in India and abroad. Their enthusiastic response, their queries and their comments have influenced the framework of the book. Grateful thanks are due to students of the Sai university; of Doon School and Rashtriya Indian Military College, Dehradun. Thanks are

also extended to senior Bal Vikas students of Delhi, of the University of Illinois at Urbana, and of the University of Pepperdine at Los Angeles; to participants in a teachers' workshop in New Jersey, USA; to an international group involved in spreading moral values at Caux, Switzerland; to student officers of the Defence Services Staff College, India, and higher command courses at the College of Combat, India; to officers of the Indian Military Academy; to participants in national management programs and executive development programs at the Management Development Institute; to numerous groups of parents and teachers in India and abroad; and to a group of American youth, who participated in the Sai university summer course on *Indian Culture and Spirituality* in 1993.

Sanjay Chibber, who has participated in the author's research since 1979, was involved in the project even as a schoolboy. He proved that living by the spirit of this book leads to deep appreciation of the individual in society and rapid success. In 1992, he became the youngest international market manager of a megacorporation in Los Angeles, U.S.A. and a role model for international business leadership. He encouraged the author with his infectious sense of humor and wisdom much beyond his years to share the results of the research with the youth of the world. Thanks to this complete earth citizen.

Grateful thanks to Dr. Narasimha Murthy of the Sai university, who carefully read the manuscript and made some excellent suggestions. Also, to Major General Bernhard Gruber of Germany; Dr. Art-Ong Jumsai Na Ayudhya of Thailand; Dr. William M. Harvey, Bill Gaum, Dr. Jack Hawley, and Hal Honig of the USA; Mr. T. R. Pillay of Canada; and Shyam Sunder of India for their comments and useful suggestions.

Mr. P. K. Raghupathy, editor of the Management Development Institute, a friend and colleague of the author, spared his time and effort to edit the manuscript and made many practical,

pragmatic suggestions to embellish the book. Deep gratitude to him for his unflinching support. Thanks also, to Mr. S. B. S. Ghuman, of the Management Development Institute, for undertaking all the secretarial work involved, with efficiency and dedication.

Grateful thanks to Judy Wechsler for editing the text for the American edition, and to Malini Angunawela for typing the new edition for *Leela Press*.

Dr. Amitabh Saraf repeatedly refined the graphics till they reached the needed quality. My sincere thanks to this spiritual scientist.

Those who understand who the Chancellor of Sai university is, and his mission, will readily appreciate that not a word of this book could have been written without his inspiration. Deep gratitude of the author—and, indeed, of all those who may benefit from the book—are due to him. He was gracious enough to write the foreword as well as the afterword for the book.

It is fervently hoped that this book will be useful to young men and women who aspire to become the leaders of tomorrow and also to parents and teachers who groom leaders.

Lt. Gen. (Dr.) M. L. Chibber

Prologue

This book has been written for youth and also for those who mold youth—parents and teachers. What is the rationale?

In the historic, but slow evolution of humanity, we are moving to a totally new age. The three centuries after 1850 are likely to be seen as an historic period in the process of changing our awareness of our own spiritual reality to a much higher level than what holds true today. We are now in the middle of this crucial period. It is fascinating to have a bird's-eye view of all that has happened in the first 150 years or so of this era of momentous transition. A brief survey indicates that the events in these one and a half centuries have been far more epoch making and significant than the entire previous history of the human race.

This period saw the culmination of humanity's attempt to conceptualize numerous ways to find the ultimate goal of peace and prosperity. All these concepts were tried, but found wanting. A variety of political systems—monarchy, dictatorship, colonialism, imperialism, fascism, socialism, communism, guided democracy and the like—were adopted in various parts of the world, but were subsequently discarded. Democracy, the best of the systems, is limping along gamely, but without achieving the declared purpose. Neither capitalism nor communism has solved the economic problems of people. Tremendous advances in science and technology have certainly made physical life very comfortable but have not added an iota to our enduring happiness. On the contrary, life has become far more stressful than ever before.

Two world wars, with their mind-boggling loss of life and property, and the subsequent cold war were fought to reach the goal of a "just world order." The phrase *just world order* was merely a term coined to lend respectability to human selfishness. At the individual level, selfishness has been made moral by calling it self-centered individualism. This shift from serving the society to serving self, has played havoc with human nature. What, then, about the remaining 150 years or so of this transition to a new age?

The challenges of the twenty-first century have been appreciated and visualized by scholars with some clinical detachment and objectivity. These will come as a traumatic shock to us. Hopefully, we will realize that, unless we rise above our petty, narrow self-interests, we may all perish. The challenges we are likely to face are:

- Demographic explosion in the world, particularly in the developing countries
- Severe economic strains produced by the marriage of the high technology and low wage, leveling the quality of life in developed and developing countries
- Ecological upheavals, which respect no national boundaries

Will the human race survive? The answer is an unqualified yes. The reason for this confident assertion is that people of vision, looking far ahead of their times, have already articulated the blueprint for human survival—nay, even for us to reach an era of peace, opportunity and plenty for all. This blueprint revolves around people leading their lives according to human values that are universally accepted by every faith and philosophy in the world. Unfortunately, for thousands of years, people have ignored this blueprint. Instead, we have pursued happiness through acquisitive greed and sensual pleasures. It is now being realized that this pursuit brings about exactly the opposite result—greed, restlessness, tension, strife, conflict and a spiritual void. This awareness is increasing and will go on spreading as we face the harder realities that lie ahead.

Among many people in India, these three centuries (up to about 2150) are being referred to as the Sai Era. During this period, a large segment of mankind is likely to graduate from religion, or from the total lack of it, to spirituality. It is likely to happen despite the determined resistance of clergies and priesthoods of various kinds and hues, who have a "bread and butter" vested interest in the status quo. This development will inevitably usher in the age of **Unity of Man, Global Economy and Earth Citizenship.**

Our transition to this unity in a mighty global state will be peaceful if the leaders learn to persuade, rather than dominate. The first essential for such leadership, as we shall discuss in this book, is selflessness. Such a foundation is perfectly possible if leaders raise their vision from self-centered individualism to promoting the welfare of humanity as a whole. Raising the vision to such a lofty height will not be easy. During recent centuries, the concept of "self-interest" of individuals, groups and nations has seeped so deeply into the human psyche that a deliberate effort and perhaps a severe jolt is needed to break its hold. Fortunately, history is full of individuals who have kept their vision of humanity, and they are the ones who have done the maximum good for mankind. Most of them at the world level are included among the 108 inspiring lives listed at the end of this book. But there are a vast number of people in every country and culture to whom the concept contained in the ancient Indian prayer *Lokaa Samastaa Sukhino Bhavantu* (meaning "may the entire world enjoy peace and plenty") is not just words, but a way of life. They have overcome their selfishness and devote their lives for the betterment of their fellow beings. Men and women in New York, London, Calcutta, Tokyo and other places silently pack some food and walk out to feed the hungry, help the distressed and bring cheer to the afflicted. They are among millions of people who have discovered by experience that unselfish service is a source of great joy. This category of people is growing.

It is from the perspective of transition of mankind to a new age that we have to take a hard look at the ancient human capability called leadership. On this quality depends the well-being, harmony and happiness of a family, society or nation. If leaders at all levels become aware of the true basis of leadership—that true leadership, which contributes to the well-being of society, is, in fact, a by-product of spirituality—then, our transition will be faster, less painful and indeed enjoyable.

This book is being written to introduce youth—the leaders of tomorrow—to some of the fundamental truths about leadership, to its practical side, and, above all, to its being a capability that can be acquired and improved upon by anyone who is prepared to make an effort to transform his or her character for the better. The book also conveys the idea that wisdom and virtue are within the reach of everyone. The fact that such qualities can be successfully acquired has been proven by determined individuals over and over again. Experience tells us that if we develop the willpower to persist, we can be the masters of our own destiny.

Parents and teachers have a special role in this great adventure of grooming effective leaders for the future, as discussed in chapter 9—teachers more than parents, because during her or his working life a teacher influences over a thousand children.

Many rationalists question the very concept of human values and selfless leadership, and call it a Utopian pipe dream. They argue, and not without pragmatic logic, that the whole approach ignores the realities that prevail in the world. Addiction to drugs, promiscuity, unethical practices and endemic violence have become part of human culture all over the world. Television, sustained by suggestive advertisements that excite our senses and encourage animality, has played havoc with society pushing it towards this decline. How can all this be reversed when prophets and saints throughout history have repeatedly been unable to change human nature, even when it was not so depraved as it is today. There is much force to this point of view, but it overlooks the evolutionary design of the Creator, which cannot be forecast by rational predictions. The sickness of modern society is so deep rooted that "it can be cured only by a spiritual revolution in the hearts and minds of human beings."[1] Hope lies in the fact that "man is capable of self-revolution."[2] After a very detailed and prolonged survey of the evolution of the human race, society and the state, Arnold Toynbee and Daisako Ikeda anticipated that, in the next chapter of history "mankind will succeed in unifying politically and spiritually."[3]

Not more than 7 to 9 percent of the human mind's potential is currently being used by us. It has such latent powers and is capable of such mighty achievements that we cannot even imagine the pinnacle to which man can climb. When faced with a choice between complete extinction and transformation, people, subconsciously perhaps, are bound to choose transformation.

Our major hope for the future is in the youth. Despite what the prophets of doom may say, much idealism exists among them—in schools, colleges and universities. And it is they who are going to be the leaders of tomorrow. This book is primarily addressed to them. They will do well to always remember that:

> The end of wisdom is freedom;
> The end of culture is perfection;
> The end of knowledge is love; and
> The end of education is character.[4]

REFERENCES

1.   Arnold Toynbee, *Choose Life*, a dialogue between Toynbee and Daisaku Ikeda (Delhi: Oxford University Press, 1987).

2.   Ikeda quoted in Toynbee, *Choose Life*.

3.   Toynbee and Ikeda.

4.   Sathya Sai Baba.

1
Introduction

It is well known that in every human activity a leader is needed to guide a group of people. In general parlance the head of a family is the most common leader. On the quality of this leader, be it the father or the mother, depends the progress, happiness and fortunes of the family.

In a modern society thousands of individuals are appointed or elected to shoulder the role and responsibilities of leadership. It happens in schools and colleges (class captains, sports team captains and captains of other activities), factories and farms, business enterprises, and dispensaries and hospitals, as well as in the civil and military organs of a country and in public life at all levels—in short, in every walk of life. If these leaders are good men or women, then they promote unity, harmony, strength, prosperity and happiness in society.

The purpose of this book is to present the leaders of tomorrow with a holistic and practical approach to leadership. Its real objective, however, is to encourage and guide them in their effort to embark on an action program of self-development so that they can improve their leadership potential to the maximum extent.

It is well to remember that leadership cannot be taught in a class. However, every individual does have the capability for self-transformation. To improve our character is one of the most challenging human activities and yet the most exciting, rewarding and joyful. We shall see how anyone who is prepared to make the necessary effort can become the master of his or her destiny!

The younger we are when we start this adventure of self-development, the higher is the level to which we can rise. We shall see in the final chapter how we acquire a number of traits while still on our mother's lap. That is why a chapter dealing with the role of parents and teachers has been included in the book.

Advice on Leadership: 5000 Years Ago

The earliest recorded treatise on good leadership is more than 5,000 years old. When we read it carefully, we realize that it may well have been articulated for leadership in today's world. It is relevant to note this famous advice on how to be a good and effective leader at the very outset.

Well before 3,000 B.C., a fierce battle depicted in the Indian scripture *Mahabharata* was fought in India on the battlefield of Kurukshetra, not too far from the modern capital of the country, Delhi.[1] It was a bloody conflict, fought between cousins—the Pandavas and Kauravas—in which the Pandavas won a total victory. In this battle lasting for 14 days, the commander in chief of the Kauravas was a grand old man named Bhishma, who at the age of 116 was loved, respected and revered by the ruling elite of both warring sides. Such was the stature of this great leader. He was severely wounded in the battle, and after his defeat he lay dying on the battlefield—his body pierced by hundreds of arrows.

Krishna, the divine guide and strategic adviser of Pandavas, took them to pay homage to Bhishma. Abandoning their chariots some distance away, they silently walked to Bhishma. Krishna then spoke to him at length, praising his great valor and sacrifice. He finally asked Bhishma to teach Yudhisthira, the eldest Pandava, the art of leadership so he could rule the vast Kingdom he had won in battle. In slow, but firm whispers, the grand old Bhishma spoke thus:

- You want to learn the art of being a leader to rule your kingdom well. I will tell you everything, my child. It was taught to me by great masters, and I will impart it all to you.

- It is not easy to rule well, and a king's one worldly duty is to rule well. It is action that shapes destiny and not the other way around.

- A king's highest duty is to the gods; next, of equal importance, is truth. Truth is the highest refuge; all the world rests on truth.

- A king's conduct should be above reproach. Self-restraint, humility, righteousness and straightforwardness are essential for his success. He should have his passions under perfect control.

- There is a danger in mildness. The king should not be too mild, or he will then be disregarded. The people will not have enough respect for him and his word. He must also avoid the other extreme, being too stringent, for then the people will be afraid of him, which is not a happy state of affairs.

- Compassion must be a part of his mental makeup, but he must guard against displaying a too forgiving nature, for then he will be considered weak by low men, who will take advantage of him.

- Alertness is essential. He must study his friends and foes all the time.

- His first duty is to his people. He should take care of them, with no thoughts of pleasing himself, subordinating his own wishes and desires to those of his people. He should guard them as a mother guards her child.

- A king needs to be careful not to place implicit confidence in anyone. He should keep his innermost thoughts concealed from even his nearest and dearest.

- If his position is weak, he needs to know when to seek protection in his fort. And he should be ready to make peace with a foe who is stronger.

- Be pleasant in speech.

- A king must surround himself with people of like nature, who have qualities that are noble. The only difference between him and his officers is the white umbrella signifying his higher office.

- The people should live in freedom and happiness, as they do in their father's house. The very essence of the king's role is to protect the people and their happiness. It is not easy to secure people's happiness. A king needs to use diverse methods. Skill, nimbleness and truth—all three are important.

- Pay attention to the state of the kingdom. Old and shabby surroundings are symbols of disregard. Renovate to win good opinion.

- Know how to use the powers of punishment, and do not hesitate to use them on miscreants. People are often led by chastisement. Know, then, the science of chastisement.

- Self-interest is the most powerful factor in the life of everyone. No one is dear to another unless there is some gain involved.

- The treasury should always be full.

- A king needs to supervise the work of all his officers himself.

- Never trust the guardians of the city or fort implicitly.
- Do things in secret from enemies. You can never protect a kingdom by candor or simplicity. A king should be both candid and wily.

- A king who is honored by his subjects will naturally be respected by his foes, and will be feared by them also.

- Nothing, not even the smallest act, can be accomplished by a single man. He has to have assistance.

- The king cannot be too careful. Wicked people may appear honest; honest ones may appear dishonest. The honest person can become dishonest, for no one can always be of the same mind.

- No one should be trusted completely. And yet a want of trust is also wrong. The policy: Trust but verify.

- A king should harbor no malice, absolutely none, in his heart.

- Dharma (right conduct) is the watchword of a king. Nothing is more powerful! To the extent he yields or diminishes dharma, to that degree disintegration sets in.

- Death is nearing every creature every moment. What you have planned to do tomorrow must be done this morning! Death is ruthless. It will never wait and see if all your projects are carried out. Readiness for it is important. The world is a passing pageant.

- A person is born alone and dies alone. He or she has not a single real companion on the march through this incident called life. The spouse, the father, the mother, sons, kinsmen, friends—all turn away from the body and go about their work. Only dharma follows the body. That is the only enduring friend a person has, and the only thing he or she should seek.

Having said all he had to say, Bhishma smiled faintly and closed his eyes, a signal for the Pandavas to go.

5

To acquire the necessary strength of character to implement Bhishma's advice, we need long and careful preparation. We must understand in practical terms the meaning of leadership, the process of leadership, the main functions of a leader, the essential components of a good leader's makeup, and the ways to strengthen these components.

Before we embark on a discussion of the above ingredients of leadership, it is important to clarify a few essential features:

- The yardstick to measure good leadership

- Leadership specific to different fields of work

- Leadership versus management

- Leadership as a by-product of spirituality

Yardstick to Measure Good Leadership

How do we measure good leadership? is a natural question that is frequently asked. People often enquire, "Wasn't Hitler a great leader? He had the whole German nation doing what he wanted them to do. German industry and technology reached new heights during his rule, and he nearly conquered the whole of Europe and North Africa." All this is true, and yet he brought untold suffering and misery on the people of Germany—indeed, to most of Europe.

The yardstick to measure good leadership is the culture of enduring excellence that a leader leaves behind after he or she is long gone from the scene.[2] This truth can be seen when we look at the culture of excellence that persists in families, institutions, business enterprises, armies, communities and even nations. Somewhere up the line a great grandfather or mother, or a chief executive or two, by dint of his or her leadership, created a culture that still endures. The world needs this type of leader to embark on an era of peace and prosperity based on the 'brotherhood of man.'

Sensing the confusion that arises in discussing the stature of various well-known leaders in history, Sathya Sai Baba, Chancellor of the Sai university, one day asked the students and teachers what was the difference between a good leader and a great leader. Various answers were offered, but none satisfied him. Finally, he conveyed the difference in these words: "A great leader is for himself, a good one is for others." Leaders like Hitler become megalomaniac and become prisoners of their ego. They are not bothered about their people. Since their main concern is themselves, they cause a great deal of suffering to their people.

Leadership Specific to a Field of Work

People often want to know how they can become good and effective leaders in their chosen field of work—for example, leadership of a sports team, a hospital, a school, a university, a service industry, a car factory, a military outfit or whatever. The answer is quite simple.

Ninety percent of leadership depends on character. The entire emphasis in the educational system of any civilization that has reached its golden age is on building character based on universal human values.

In these civilizations, students are constantly reminded about this cardinal need, with great emphasis. The entire curriculum of studies and other activities in educational institutions is geared towards this goal. Thus, sound character is common to leadership in all fields of work and forms 90 percent of our potential. If we add the remaining 10 percent as knowledge about the chosen field of work, then we become leaders in that particular field. For example, the effectiveness of a general depends 90 percent on his character and 10 percent on his professional knowledge and ability in the art of war. Similarly, the effectiveness of a business leader depends 90 percent on his character and 10 percent on his knowledge of managing a business.

There is an interesting finding by the Stanford Research Institute in the USA, which has bearing on the issue. During the eighties, many scholars in that country began to investigate why the Japanese were forging ahead of them in almost every economic enterprise and activity. This was happening in spite of the Japanese not having many colleges teaching business management in their country; whereas, the Americans had some of the best business management colleges in the world.

The findings of the Stanford Research Institute pinpointed an area the Americans had ignored. In its report, the institute virtually sums up the composition of good leadership that has to be rediscovered. The study concluded that:

> Twelve percent of effective management [management terminology for *leadership*] is knowledge and eighty-eight percent is dealing appropriately with people.[3]

We will notice in this book that it is essentially the character of a leader that enables him to deal appropriately with people. No superficially acquired skill can replace this fundamental truth. Ralph Waldo Emerson, the famous American author, voiced this universal fact when he said: "What you are shouts so loudly in my ears that I cannot hear what you say."

Leadership and Management

There is often a futile argument about what is more important—leadership or management.

Ever since the French Revolution many scholars have viewed leadership as undemocratic. Leadership was considered by them to be a misused privilege of the aristocracy and feudal lords who dominated human civilization at that stage of history. The very concept of leadership became suspect in the eyes of the academic community. They argued that democracy meant equality for all; hence, there was no need for leadership. This was a mistaken view.

Democracy means equality of opportunity and not equality of capability. Even two brothers with a common heritage who grow up in a common environment have different capabilities. But the reluctance about leadership persisted—particularly in France and the USA, which adopted equality as one of the major pillars of its constitution.

With the development of management as a social science in the universities, the concept of leadership received a further setback. The watershed in this trend was reached when, during the seventies, even the armed forces of the USA replaced the concept of leadership with management. This happened during the period when Robert McNamara was U.S. secretary of defence. The country was then involved in the Vietnam War. The Americans lost that war—the only war they have lost in their history. One major reason for the defeat was that they had discarded leadership in favor of management. They have since learned their lesson and have restored the emphasis on leadership as the key factor in winning wars.

It is well to appreciate that management is a very useful tool in the hands of a leader. One can be a good manager without being a leader, but one cannot be a good leader without being a good manager. In fact, it is wrong even to start comparing the two. However, since there has been so much controversy, it is useful to quote the elder statesmen of management in the United States.

> Management is a bottom line focus. How can I best accomplish certain things? Leadership deals with the

top line. What things I want to accomplish. In the words of both Peter Drucker and Warren Bennis:—"Management is doing things right; leadership is doing the right things." Management efficiency is in climbing the ladder of success; leadership determines whether the ladder is leaning against the right wall.[4]

In an analysis of management eras during the current century, the 1990s have been designated as the "Era of Leadership." This development emphasizes the rediscovery of leadership as the key factor in the excellence of families, organizations, communities, nations—indeed the world. It is, therefore, appropriate that youth should learn about this human capability.

Leadership is a By-product of Spirituality

As we progress in our discussion of leadership, it will become clear that it is a by-product of spirituality. Yet this truth is of such fundamental importance that it merits our attention at the very beginning. By practicing it, Indian civilization has been able to survive for over 6,000 years. This point was forcefully made by the Chancellor of the Sai university in November 1991.

It was the eve of opening a superspecialty hospital, a unique institution providing free major surgery on all internal organs. This hospital of gigantic size, with beautiful architectural design and state-of-the-art equipment from all over the world, was being worked on round the clock. There was tremendous excitement among people gathered from various countries to watch this event. One morning the Chancellor of the university came and stood near the postgraduate students. He was carrying a letter in his hand.

In a casual manner he mentioned to the students that the letter was from the president of India. The president had been the guest of honor a year ago when the foundation stone of the hospital was

10

laid and the chancellor declared that the hospital would start functioning exactly a year later. For a variety of reasons, the construction work could not start for about six months. The project finally began when the chancellor intervened, and now it was about to be completed on schedule.

The president of India had written in the letter that completion of the project in five months was a miracle. If this project were to be undertaken by the government of India, it would take at least five years to complete!

The Chancellor was about to walk away when the author, sitting nearby, said that this achievement would make an excellent case study on leadership for the M.B.A. students of the university. The Chancellor paused, looked hard at the author and said, "No, it is not management" and then, raising his eyes to the far horizons, he recited the ancient Sanskrit sloka from Vedas, given to humanity thousands of years ago:

> *Na Karmana, na prajaya, dhanena, Thyagenaike*
> *amrutatwa manshu.* [Not by action, not by progeny,
> not by wealth, but by sacrifice alone can immortality
> be achieved.]

Thyaga is the key element in this stanza. It is not easy to translate this Sanskrit word into English. Its sense is contained in sacrifice, selflessness and renunciation of self-interest. It is this virtue that enables a leader to achieve the impossible.

But what is spirituality? And what is self-realization?

Spirituality is rising above religions marked by purely ceremonial aspects of church, mosque or temple. It is understanding and then experiencing that the creator and his creation are ONE.

The following observation by Sai Baba makes the process and the end of spiritual growth absolutely clear:

> It is good to be born in a religion, but not good to die in one. Grow and rescue yourself from the limits of regulations, doctrines that fence in your freedom of thought, and ceremonies and rites that restrict and direct. Reach the point where churches do not matter, where all roads end from where all roads began.[5]

Spiritual growth can be achieved if we live our worldly life in accordance with human values. Spiritual growth culminates in the experience of our reality. This universal experience has been described by saints and seers of all faiths:

> "I and my father are one."—Christianity
> "Annul Haqq. [I am the truth.]"—Islam
> "So Ham. [I am that.]"—Hinduism

Note for Teachers

It is easier for students to understand leadership if the contents of this book are related to a real-life situation. For example, one teacher started the study by having the students assume that each one was selected to captain the college sports team of his or her choice. The captain was required to select, train and develop the team so that it would win the intercollege tournament to be held in about six months.

Another teacher, who had class 11 students, asked them to assume that each one would be selected as head boy/head girl of the school when promoted to class 12.

Numerous variations could be used to give students a leadership role.

2

Leadership Defined: Process and Functions of Leadership

Definition of Leadership

There are more than 350 definitions for the word *Leadership* in academic literature in the English language alone. It indicates the general confusion that prevails about the subject and also its complexity.

The definition that has a touch of practical common sense is the one evolved by Lord Moran of Britain, a doctor who was the medical officer in a British infantry battalion during World War I (1914-1918) in France.

He saw how young army officers, hardly out of school, inspired their fellow citizens to fight the Germans, both in attack and defense, knowing fully well that many among them would get killed or maimed. He started to wonder how one man could exercise such decisive influence over others. For a while he thought that it was due to the authority and rank given to officers or the stringent military law used to enforce spartan military discipline. But in spite of the rank and military discipline, he also started to witness examples of demeaning cowardice when officers were just not able to persuade their troops to risk their lives. The war ended and Moran went back to his profession. In 1939, on the eve of World War II, Moran had risen to become the president of the British Medical Council—virtually the world's number one doctor at that stage of history. He was also appointed as the personal physician to Sir Winston Churchill, the wartime prime minister of Britain. In that capacity he had a ringside seat for observing the top leaders of the world in every human activity—politics, industry, military affairs, labor and so on. Given below is a definition based on what he evolved:

> Leadership is the capacity to frame plans that will succeed and the faculty to persuade others to carry them out in the face of all difficulties—even death.

The definition has two parts. The first deals with the capacity to frame plans (programs, projects or whatever) that have a high probability of success. It implies that the plan should be realistic. To be so, a leader should have full information about the size and quality of his or her resources. The leader should also understand the environments in which the plan has to be implemented. The second part of the definition deals with implementation. No plan can ever be implemented exactly as originally conceived. It has to be implemented by those who are working for their leader. They are bound to face difficulties and obstacles. They are bound to have their own ideas about the task in hand. That is why a leader has to have the faculty to persuade others to implement the plan despite difficulties, discouragements and setbacks. It is this capability, which, as we have discussed earlier, amounts to 88 percent of the effectiveness of a leader.

In normal parlance the definition we have adopted can be expressed in very simple terms. In any situation, no matter at what level or how complex, leadership amounts to:

Knowing what to do + Getting things done

The difference in the size of letters in the two parts indicates the relative importance of the two components. To make a realistic plan is important. But to get it implemented is a far more important and challenging capability of a leader. Sound knowledge of the field of our work helps us in deciding what to do, and the strength of our character helps us in getting things done. In management terminology, the definition can be expressed as:

Capability + **Effectiveness**

What type of person can measure up to the definition of leadership we have adopted?

In the recent five or six decades, there has been a frantic search for "quick fix" and "instant" techniques for creating effective leaders (managerial effectiveness is the term used for leadership in management literature). Persuasive books on leadership theories, styles, attitudes, behavior, tools and techniques have been marketed for aspiring leaders.

In this quest for short cuts, at long last, it is now being realized that there is no easy or quick recipe for becoming a good and effective leader. This realization has been very cogently expressed in these words. "If I try to use human influence, strategies and tactics ... to get other people to do what I want ... while my character is fundamentally flawed, marked by duplicity and insincerity, then, in the long run, I cannot be successful."[2] It is in relation to this problem that the Indian experience of surviving for 6,000 years as a civilization with cycles of great glory and deep deprivation has much relevance to our study.

In November 1990, Sathya Sai Baba, the Chancellor of the Sai university, had a long interaction with the M.B.A. students and teachers. Being a stickler for perfection in every field of education at the University, he questioned them at great length about the leadership course and what they had learned from it. After discussion for about an hour, he gave conceptual clarity to two fundamental issues related to leadership:

- Who can be a good leader?

- What does the leadership process involve?

15

Who Can Be a Good Leader?

Only a person whose thoughts, words and deeds are in harmony can become a good and effective leader. His or her thoughts are pure; their source is not related to lust, anger, attachment, greed, egotism or jealousy. Such leaders say what they think (there is no duplicity in that), and they do what they say (there is no insincerity or hypocrisy in their deeds). In brief, they are transparent and straightforward people in word and conduct. Diagrammatically, two persons are depicted in figure 2.1. The first one is a clever worldly person whose thoughts are related to self-interest. Such a person thinks one thing but says something different and when it comes to doing, will seldom do what he or she has promised. The second person has harmony of thought, word and deed.

We trust a person whose thoughts, words and deeds are in harmony. It is this type of person who has the potential for becoming a good leader. In later chapters we shall discuss the character of such a person in more detail.

The Leadership Process: *"The Mahavakya"*

The leadership discussion at the Sai university culminated in the Chancellor articulating what has come to be known as the *mahavakya* (the great utterance*) on leadership. He summed up the entire distillate of the leadership process in just eight words:

---

*Mahavakya is the term used for the short and crisp eternal truths articulated in the most ancient literature of humanity—the Vedas. Aldous Huxley, using one of these truths, "thou art that" as his theme, wrote his seminal book *The Perennial Philosophy.*

HARMONY IN
THOUGHT, WORD AND DEED

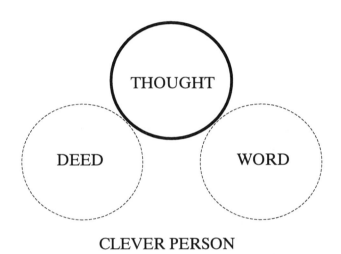

CLEVER PERSON

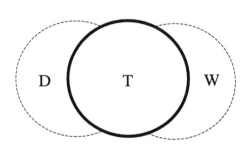

TRUSTWORTHY PERSON

Figure 2.1

TO BE, TO DO, TO SEE, TO TELL

Diagrammatically, the *mahavakya* and the relative importance of its components are shown in figure 2.2.

TO BE is the source of leadership.

TO DO is the style of leadership by personal example.

TO SEE and TO TELL are the functions, tools and techniques of leadership.

To be means the aggregate of all there is in a person. It is composed of the person's values, qualities and knowledge. In other words, his or her total being. "*To be* is the beginning and the end of leadership."[3]

This simple sentence conveys the historic truth that the potential and effectiveness of a leader is in direct proportion to the strength of his *to be*. That is why in figure 2.2, *to be* is shown as the largest component in the leadership process. For this very reason the holistic and practical approach to leadership expounded in this book lays a major emphasis on *to be*. The universal constituents of the *to be* of a good and effective leader are explained in chapters 3, 4, 5 and 6, while the techniques to reinforce them are discussed in chapters 7 and 8. However, it is appropriate to restate that 90 percent of the *to be* of a leader is his or her character.

To do indicates that the best style of leadership is to lead by personal example, to practice what we preach. Style is the reflection of our substance—our total being. Personal example can be set only if the *to be* of the leader is worthy of emulation. Phonies who pretend to be what they are not are very quickly found out—"You can smell them from a mile away."[4] In

LEADERSHIP PROCESS

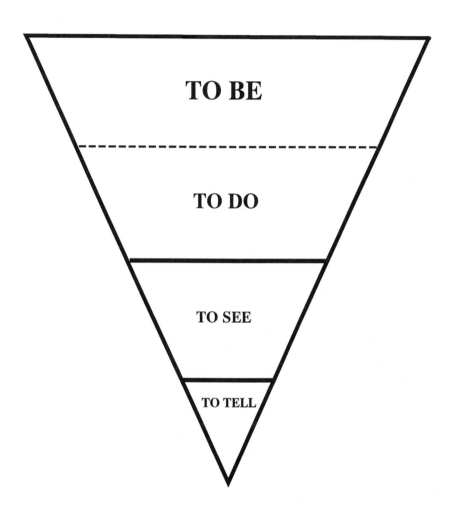

TO BE

TO DO

TO SEE

TO TELL

Figure   2.2

figure 2.2, this reality is depicted by a perforated line between to be and *to do*. Mahatma Gandhi set a personal example in eradicating untouchability by mixing and eating in homes of untouchables. Personal example, in peace and in war, is transparent and most infectious. It is the most potent technique for influencing people. It is rightly called the method of silent persuasion. Three examples will illustrate what is involved in practicing what we preach.

Dr. V. Gokak was the first vice chancellor (chief executive) of the Sai university. He was also the chairman of the Sahitya (Literature) Academy of India at Delhi—a great honor for a man of letters. When his term with the academy expired, the well-known poet Professor Bannarji was appointed to succeed him. Because of hectic activity at the university, Dr. Gokak was unable to go to Delhi. So the members of the governing body of the academy, along with Professor Bannarji, came down to Prasanthi Nilayam to perform the formality of handing over the reins—taking over the chairmanship of the academy. After they arrived, the Chancellor invited them all into his interview room.

As soon as they were seated, Professor Bannarji took out a handkerchief from his pocket. "It was a dirty and stinking bundle of cloth," recalled the Chancellor, as he was narrating the story after explaining the meaning of *to do*. He continued, "In fact it was almost black. I soon realized why Bannarji was carrying this lump of garbage in his pocket. He was addicted to inhaling snuff. After inhaling the black powder, he would blow his nose into the handkerchief. That was the cause of the dirt he was carrying. I advised him that inhaling snuff was a bad addiction and that he should give it up. Bannarji listened to me in respectful silence. And then, at that very moment, I wiped my mouth and looked at my own handkerchief. It was covered all over with red marks. Those were the days when I used to chew pan (betel leaf) virtually round the clock. Looking at my handkerchief, I asked myself a question. What was the difference between Bannarji's addiction and my own addiction? Both were bad habits. How could I advise Bannarji when I myself was a victim of a similar vice. I resolved, there and then, that I would not touch pan again. It is more than 10 years since I have chewed pan. Of course, Bannarji also threw away his snuff box as soon as he left the interview room."

In the second example, we shall see what happens when we do not practice what we preach. This example is from a war between India and a neighboring country.

Brig. Mohmad Latif of the Indian Army launched an attack to capture an enemy-held hilltop nicknamed Baldy. The surrounding hilly terrain of the objective was covered with dense pine forest. Brig. Latif selected the Guards Battalion for this tough task.

As is shown in figure 2.3, the attack involved going down into a valley and then climbing up to capture Baldy. It took the Guards the full day to clear the outposts guarding approaches to the objective. It was nearing dusk when Baldy was finally captured.

Hardly had the commander of the Guards finished reporting his success on the radio when Brig. Latif, watching through his binoculars, noticed a major counterattack moving towards Baldy. He could see hundreds of enemy soldiers moving through the pines on the ridge leading to Baldy. It was a disturbing development because the Guards were hardly organized to face a major counterattack. They had fought the whole day, suffered casualties, were short of ammunition, and had eaten just one meal. Brig. Latif warned the Guards to get ready, and soon artillery shelling started from both sides. Brig. Latif was mentally prepared to lose Baldy because it was a very unequal fight.

When the counterattacking forces were about 400 yards from Baldy, the Guards opened up with their machine guns. To the utter surprise and relief of Brig. Latif, within minutes the entire

CAPTURE OF BALDY

1971 WAR

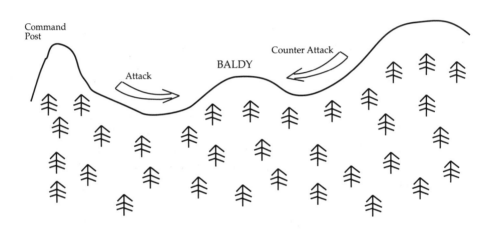

Figure 2.3

counterattack petered away. He could not believe his eyes but congratulated the Guards for their performance.

A little while later the Guards reported that they had captured two unwounded prisoners. The brigadier ordered that they be sent to his command post immediately, since he wanted to personally interrogate them to try to get information for finalizing his plans for subsequent operations.

The pair arrived at the command post almost at midnight. One was a young soldier in his teens. He was so scared that he could not speak at all. The other was a corporal and a very talkative fellow. He gave out more information than Brig. Latif really needed. Towards the end of his interrogation, the brigadier asked the corporal, "You seem to be a seasoned soldier. How come you gave yourself up when you were not even wounded?—not a very honorable action for a good soldier." The corporal was more than willing to explain and tell his story.

"Our commander was right in front when the counterattack started. Holding his Sten gun in his one hand, he encouraged us to wipe out your troops and recapture Baldy. He was inspiring us by loud talk. His booming voice could be heard all over. He was a towering personality. We were determined and enthusiastic to finish the task. We kept on advancing even when your shelling started. When your troops opened up fire with machine guns, our commander immediately took cover behind the trunk of a huge pine tree. Standing in that sheltered position, he waved his Sten gun and ordered us to rush forward and destroy the enemy. We did rush forward, but very soon we also started taking shelter behind the pine trees. I was unlucky enough to be captured by your patrol before I could slip away down the slope, like the others and return to our base."

Here was a sure victory on the plate for the counterattacking force, but the commander was unable to set the right example.

Good or bad, the personal example of a leader is most infectious. It is because of this that a Persian saying conveys a very naked truth:

> If the king plucks one apple from the public garden,
> the public will take away even the roots.

The third example of *to do* is also from a war. The Indian Army assisted the Bangladesh forces in liberating their country from Pakistan in 1971. After the war, there was serious concern among the senior officers of the Fifth Gorkha Rifles—a crack regiment of the army. The Fourth Battalion of the regiment was fighting in Bangladesh. After the cease-fire, this battalion suffered 65 percent officer casualties in just 14 days of war. The older officers were concerned about this very high rate of attrition. Was there something wrong with the battalion? If there was, then it must be set right immediately. Regimental honor must not be blemished on any account. However, the cause of concern soon disappeared.

The reason for the very high attrition was that there developed a competition in gallantry among the officers. It all started with the commanding officer, Colonel Harolikar. Wherever there was danger, he was physically present on the spot, leading his troops from the front. The battalion fought its battle with elan and great gusto. Very naturally, it was selected for the riskiest and the toughest operation of that war. It was lifted by helicopters and landed behind a Pakistani brigade at Sylhet. The battalion isolated the enemy brigade from its base at Dacca. The brigade did its best to destroy the Gorkhas. But, by now, the officers were competing in gallantry and held the enemy at bay for three nights and three days. There was no way the Gorkhas could be dislodged. The enemy brigade withdrew. The action opened up a direct land route to Dacca. As a result, the war ended in just 14 days.

Not only did the battalion win numerous gallantry awards, but it was also instrumental in hastening the final victory. All this happened because the commanding officer led his troops by personal example of courage and gallantry.

To see implies that leaders must be in complete touch with the realities of the environments in which they are working. They should have the fullest possible information regarding the problem or the task to be handled. Only then can they evaluate the options that they have open to them to make a sound decision and evolve a realistic plan of action. *Seeing* involves going out to actually get a feel for things on the spot "You cannot sit in an air-conditioned office and make decisions."[5]

Decision making is a capability for which very detailed programs of teaching are available. In the military, it is called appreciation or estimate of the situation. In management education, it is called decision making and results in a project report. The essential ingredients in this process are:

- Being absolutely clear about the goal that has to be achieved

- Collecting and evaluating all relevant information about human and material resources available for the task, environments in which the task has to be carried out, opposition and obstacles likely to be met, and time available for completing the task

- Crystallizing the options that emerge from the evaluated information and examining the advantages vis-à-vis the disadvantages of each option

- Finally, selecting an option and formulating a plan or a project for implementation

It is, basically, a common sense process that we subconsciously adopt in performing almost every task—crossing a street, getting a team ready for a tournament, undertaking a journey, buying a house, setting up a business or factory, or fighting a battle. It is seldom that a clear-cut option with all the advantages emerges from the process. There are always uncertainties and imponderables, which in the art of war is called the fog of war—unforeseeable developments, human frailty and so on. That is why, as we shall discuss later in the book, courage to decide is a very important quality of a leader's character.

To see is even more important at the implementation stage of any work. There are always difficulties and obstacles in the way of carrying out a task. Therefore, proper feedback and seeing the progress of work on the spot is absolutely essential. Then only can a leader show others how to overcome problems. Thus only can he make sound decisions to modify the plan or reallocate resources or whatever. *To tell* means conveying to others what the leader wants them to do. Telling is effective if the instructions of the leader are clearly understood. This happens when the channel of communication is through the heart and depends entirely on the strength of the *to be* and the *to do* of the leader. If he has good qualities and sound knowledge, and he leads by personal example, then very few words are necessary to convey what a leader wants done.

The skill of good communication is taught by experts with a great deal of professional capability. In many postgraduate programs there are up to three full-credit courses devoted to this skill. But in the final analysis character communicates more eloquently than anything we say or do.

The entire process of leadership is held together by one virtue in a leader—selfless love. It is always useful to remember a well-known comment on selfless love:

> Love lives by giving and forgiving; self lives by getting and forgetting.[6]

The relevance of these words becomes clear when we see how a person has to carry people with him when he functions as a leader.

Functions of Leadership

In practical terms leaders have to achieve the task (mission, objective or goal). For doing so, they have to build their team as a cohesive group and develop every individual in the team to give his or her very best. Consequently, they have to harmonize and integrate the needs related to the accomplishment of the task with those of the group they lead and individuals in the group. We shall discuss in some detail how to deal with people in a later chapter. But leaders have to be absolutely clear about the needs of the three parties involved. This is best explained diagrammatically by depicting these needs in three linked circles, as shown in figure 2.4.[7]

Functions for Task Needs

- Defining the task

- Making the plan

- Allocating work and resources

- Controlling quality and tempo of work

Functions for Team Needs

- Setting standards by personal example

- Maintaining discipline, correcting mistakes

- Building team spirit

- Encouraging, motivating, and giving a sense of purpose

FUNCTIONS
OF LEADERSHIP

Figure   2.4

- Appointing subleaders

- Ensuring communication within the group

- Training the group

Functions for Individual Needs

- Attending to personal problems

- Praising of individuals

- Knowing individuals personally

- Recognizing and using special individual abilities

- Training individuals

The functions related to the needs of the three areas have been listed separately for easy understanding. In actual practice, however, most of these are integrated in the following steps:

- Being crystal clear about the task to be achieved

- Planning to achieve the task by using available resources and people

- Controlling by monitoring the work, modifying the plan if necessary

- Supporting by encouragement, recognition and training people, and evaluating to learn lessons so that performance can be improved

Note for Teachers

Real-life stories of leaders achieving great goals by personal example motivate youth a great deal. These should be carefully selected from local history and lore known to the students.

Functions of leadership may be discussed with students in relation to the leadership role allotted to them for the purposes of this study, as suggested in the introduction.

3
To Be: The Universal Inner Structure of Good Leaders: The Foundation

When we study and analyze outstanding leaders in history who have done some lasting good for the human race, a nation, a community, an organization or a cause, we find that they are not similar. They come in all shapes and hues—the flamboyant, the scholarly, the artistic, the ascetic, the gregarious and the recluse. And yet, when we use common sense to look deeper into their makeup, we find something interesting. There *to be* component, in one way or the other, is very strong. They have two things in common:

- They are all persons of character.

- They have an inner structure that is composed of certain universal qualities.

Before we take a look at the universal qualities common to all good leaders, we have to be quite clear in our mind about the frequently used word *character*.

What is Character?

Each individual is a bundle of virtues and weaknesses of head and heart. The individuality resulting from this balance sheet of good and bad qualities is that person's character.

Historically, the strength of a person's character has been the indicator of his or her potential for leadership. However, researchers in leadership were unable to define and confine the

31

qualities of leadership within the parameters of research methodology. Consequently, "like the hard questions in an examination paper, the research scholars have continually deferred them to some future date."[1] The famous scholar Stogdill is supposed to have been responsible for promoting the concept that character qualities do not play much part in leadership. This, in fact, is not true. He had merely deferred his research on character qualities. He "once told me that he never intended to close off research on the personality (meaning character) of leaders (he hoped to focus it better), but that is what happened."[2]

It is time that this purely academic confusion is removed. Character is the most important factor making for effective leaders. However, we have to describe a person of character with some clarity, so that there is a well-defined model based on historical experience.

Two descriptions of a person of character should provide the necessary clarity. The first one is by a western journalist having a deep understanding of people and matters, both in the West and India. She spent many years in India and took an interest in Indian culture. She describes a person of character (a gentleman or a lady in the true sense of the word) as:

> An honest man;
>
> a man with a sense of duties and obligations of his position, whatever it may be;
>
> a man who tells the truth;
>
> a man who gives to others their due;
>
> a man considerate to the weak;
>
> a man who has principles and stands by them;
>
> a man not too elated by good fortune and not too depressed by bad;

a man who is loyal;

a man who can be trusted.[3]

Quite obviously, an individual of character is a person who practices human values. The second description is by a seasoned and highly respected leader, General Mathew B. Ridgway of the U.S. Army. A veteran of World War II and a highly decorated officer, he rose to become the supreme commander of the UN forces in Korea and was also the chairman of the Joint Chiefs of Staff. He says:

> Character stands for self-discipline, loyalty, readiness to accept responsibility, and willingness to admit mistakes. It stands for selflessness, modesty, humility, willingness to sacrifice when necessary and, in my opinion, faith in God. Let me illustrate.
>
> During a critical phase of the Battle of the Bulge in World War II, the Germans launched a counter-offensive and nearly broke through the Allied lines in France. When I commanded the 18th Airborne Corps, another Corps Commander just entering the fight next to me remarked—"I am glad to have you on my flank. It's character that counts." I had long known him and knew what he meant. I replied "that goes for me too." There was no amplification; none was necessary. Each knew that the other would stick to it, however great the pressure; would extend help before it was asked, if he could; and would tell the truth; seek no self-glory, and everlastingly keep his word. Such men breed confidence and success.[4]

Once again, it is more than clear that a person of character practices human values, and his thoughts, words and deeds are in harmony. In order to drive home the point, it would be appropriate to look at an example of a person who lacks character.

A consultant was told by a manager in a paint factory about his boss:—"I do not trust him, nor does anyone else. He is a slick operator, out to get to the very top. He says one thing to your face and another behind your back. He doesn't actually lie, but he deals in half truths."[4] Here was a man dedicated totally to self-advancement. This boss, when confronted by the consultant, dismissed leadership as 'kidology' and added, "why should I tell the truth to my people on the way up, when I do not intend to come down again."[5]

This is an example from an enterprise in the United Kingdom, but the whole world is getting a large number of such self-centered "climbers." In the long run, they are doing a great deal of damage to their enterprises because they lack character.

One more factor has prevented the necessary focus on character from being the main source of leadership. It is the very large number of character qualities attributed to each individual. For example, Napoleon listed 90 qualities that are necessary in a good leader. Recently, the Government of India wanted to introduce education in human values in the Indian schools. They appointed a high-power committee to list the values that should be taught to the children. The committee produced a list of 154 values for the purpose! Little wonder that research scholars have been shying away from sticking their neck out to identify qualities that make a person a good leader. Fortunately, there is a way out.

When we use common sense and clinical detachment to study the lives of outstanding leaders, we find something very interesting. All of them have a few qualities of character and knowledge that are universal. When we take an integrated look at these qualities, they form a cohesive structure that diagrammatically looks as shown in figure 3.1.

It is a balanced structure in which every component of *character* and *knowledge* supports one another. This balance varies with every leader. However, it is appropriate to understand that both character and knowledge are necessary for their balance. Mere knowledge without strength of character makes a man indecisive. Mere character not supported by knowledge puts a ceiling on a leader's potential. On the *strength* and *balance* of this structure depend the effectiveness of a leader. His self-confidence is related to this balance. Self-confidence makes a leader proactive, which means that "We are responsible for our own lives. Our behavior is a function of our decisions, not our condition. We can subordinate feelings to values. We have the initiative and responsibility to make things happen.[6] Anyone who wishes to develop his or her leadership potential to the maximum should carefully study this structure. We shall discuss in a later chapter how to strengthen it.

Let us first of all take a thorough look at the foundation of leadership—selflessness. It would be appropriate to do so in the prevailing world situation. We are living in an age when "self-interest" has become the goal of life. It is not surprising, therefore, that many people are reluctant to accept selflessness as the foundation of leadership—it makes them feel very uncomfortable.

Selflessness: The Foundation of Leadership

"Selfishness is human, selflessness is divine"[7] is the truth about this noble virtue. It is the fountainhead of all that is good and moral in a human being.

As shown in figure 3.1, selflessness (call it unselfishness or sacrifice if you will) is based on an ideal or a vision an individual has as his or her goal in life. The higher the vision, the higher the degree of selflessness; thus, the higher the potential for leadership is virtually a law. And yet there is an enormous resistance among people to accept this truth. There is a very perceptive observation

UNIVERSAL INNER STRUCTURE
OF GOOD LEADERS

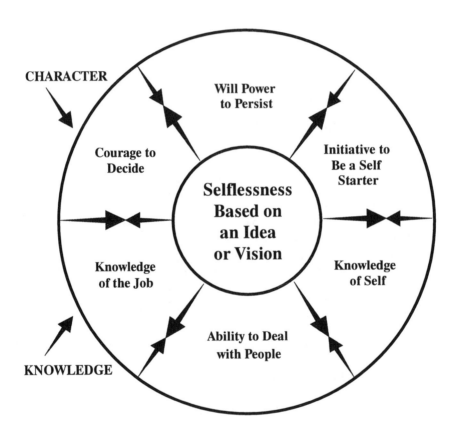

Figure 3.1

about this reality by Swami Vivekananda: "I cannot ask everybody to be totally selfless: it is not possible. But, if you cannot think of humanity at large, at least think of your country. If you cannot think of your country, think of your community. If you cannot think of your community, think of your family. If you cannot think of your family, at least think of your wife. For heaven's sake do not think merely of yourself."[8] A whole spectrum of ideals have been mentioned.

At the lowest end is "I, me and mine," and at the highest, "humanity." It is obvious that selflessness is a relative quality. Total selflessness is a rather rare phenomenon. But it does exist. When we look for examples of people who were completely selfless and lived for humanity at large, we see Rama, Krishna, Buddha, Jesus, Prophet Muhammad, Guru Nanak, Ramakrishna and the like. The most significant characteristic of these people is that they continue to have a tremendous impact on the minds of others even after many centuries.

If we analyze selflessness, its diagrammatic composition can be depicted as in figure 3.2.

Central to the virtue of selflessness is faith—faith in God, conscience, the inner voice or whatever. It has been described by the chancellor of the Sai university as a person's life breath. It gives us:

self-confidence; then

self-satisfaction; then

self-sacrifice; and finally,

self-realization.

Selflessness is also the repository of all that is noble in a human being. The five most important human values are included in the diagram. These are briefly explained below:

COMPOSITION OF SELFLESSNESS
THE SOURCE OF HUMAN VALUES

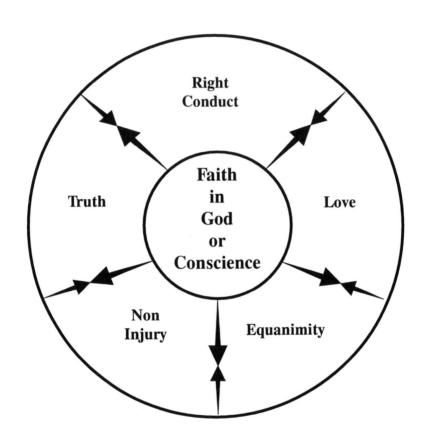

Figure 3.2

- Truth—that which does not change. In Sanskrit it is called *sathya*.

- Right Conduct—conduct that befits the duties and obligations of a person's position, whatever it may be. In Sanskrit it is called *dharma*.

- Love—unselfish love that expects nothing in return. In Sanskrit it is called *prema*.

- Equanimity—perfect peace of mind. In Sanskrit it is called *shanti*.

- Noninjury—not hurting anyone by word or deed. In Sanskrit it is called *ahimsa*.

Out of the five values discussed above, the first two, truth and right conduct, virtually contain the distillate of all morality. Honesty, integrity and loyalty are inherent in them. There is—an ancient Indian edict based on these two—*Sathyam Vada, Dharmam Chara.* It translates as "speak the truth and act as appropriate to the duties and obligations of your position, whatever it may be." And when one acts with unselfish love, then there is perfect peace and equanimity in success or failure, pleasure or pain, joy or grief.

Selfless people are neither greedy nor looking for shortcuts to success; hence, their integrity never wavers. They seek no unfair advantage over others; hence, honesty comes naturally to them. They are not self-seekers; hence, their loyalty is steady and strong. When people have these virtues, then their thoughts, words and deeds become well integrated. They say what they think and do what they say. There is no "double speak" in their nature. That establishes their credibility, and they are trusted. Trustworthy people alone can become leaders.

In spite of what has been said about selflessness, it runs totally contrary to the current culture of cutthroat competition and the rat race to get ahead. The goal of life is to rise fast in a career and get rich overnight. Consequently, it needs very deliberate reflection on the part of potential leaders to understand that the effectiveness of a leader does depend on selflessness. It is necessary, therefore, to discuss this virtue in greater detail.

The most remarkable example of how selflessness among leaders contributes to building great organizations can be found in Germany. It is a universally accepted fact that, in spite of suffering defeats in World Wars I and II, the German army was the best military force involved in the two wars. Even up to the bitter end of World War II in 1945, it did not lose its cohesive balance, fighting spirit and dedicated efficiency. How was this feat achieved?

A scholar studying the German general staff asked Field Marshal Von Moltke about the qualities that they looked for while selecting officers for the general staff. He was eager to learn this, as the general staff provided the key elements of leadership to the German army. The aging field marshal reflected for a while and replied: "The first has not been so much the possession of any quality as the absence of a quality—the quality of ambition. When with us, if an officer is a climber (one who is interested mainly in self-advancement)—we have no further use of him."[9] They had adopted selflessness as the cardinal virtue officers needed to be members of the general staff. They had merely adopted a truth known to man since the dawn of history. The following two points need to be discussed in connection with the validity of this statement:

- Evidence of history that selflessness does in fact count.

- Ways good leaders can be without ambition.

Evidence of History: Importance of Selflessness

We would focus our attention on three views recorded in three different cultures: the most recent from Europe, then from China, and the oldest from India.

Dr. Victor E. Frankel is an Austrian psychiatrist. A man of Jewish descent, he lived through the German concentration camps and survived. As a psychiatrist, he is being classed with Freud and Jung. Let us very carefully ponder over his famous words:

> Again and again, I admonish my students in Europe and America: Don't aim at success—the more you aim at it, and make it a target, the more you are going to miss it. For success, like happiness, cannot be pursued; it must ensue, and it only does so, as the unintended side-effect of one's personal dedication to a cause greater than oneself, or as the by-product of one's surrender to a person other than oneself. Happiness must happen and the same holds for success; You have to let it happen by not caring about it. I want you to listen to what your conscience commands you to do and go on to carry it out to the best of your knowledge. Then you will live to see that, in the long run—in the long run, I say: "Success will follow you precisely because you had forgotten to think about it."[10]

Let us now go back about 2,000 years. The famous Chinese scholar Lao-tzu articulated the value of selflessness for a leader in the following pragmatic words; it would appear that he, perhaps, was thinking of our times when he wrote them! Note his emphasis on the self-interest of a leader.

41

True self interest teaches selflessness.
Heaven and Earth endure because they are not simply
selfish, but endure on behalf of all creations.
The wise leader, knowing this, keeps egocentricity in
check and, by doing so, becomes even more effective.
Enlightened leadership is service not selfishness.
The leader grows more and lasts longer by placing the
well-being of all above the well-being of self alone.[11]

And finally, let us go back about 5,000 years. That was the time
the *Bhagavad-Gita*, the well-known book on spirituality, was
articulated on the battlefield of Kurukshetra in the *Mahabharata*.
The concept of *nishkama karma* was highlighted. It means doing
one's work with dedication without being bothered about benefits
it will bring. The concept has a sound basis. It is the expectation
and hope for benefits that is the major cause of worry, anxiety and
restlessness, with the result that this agitation of mind adversely
affects our performance. If we play tennis with an eye on the
scoreboard, then there is a good chance that we will start missing
the ball. On the other hand, if we maintain our concentration on
the ball, then we will play the best game that we can. The words
of Dr. Victor E. Frankel on the secret of success are virtually a
paraphrase of this ancient truth. The reader will do well to go
back and reread what he has to say.

Ambition and Leadership

We saw how the German general staff weeded out ambitious
officers—ambitious for self-advancement, the climbers. There is
a widespread belief that ambition is a good motive force for
achievement, that without ambition a person becomes inert and
placid. Consequently, how can we conceive a leader without
ambition? Was the German general staff made up of faceless men
with no fire in their bellies? These are legitimate and logical
doubts and should be discussed.

The dictionary meaning of the word *ambition* is "aspiration for success or advancement." It is true that ambition is a powerful motivator. People eager for personal success and advancement are dynamic and produce very good short-term results. However, it is those who are driven by ambition for an ideal or a vision higher than themselves who really achieve enduring results. Four hundred years ago, Francis Bacon, the great English analyst of human nature, wrote about ambitious men. The classic words in which he described an ambitious person are as true today as they were then. He observes (the meaning of some of the old words are in brackets):

> Ambition is like choler [biliousness], which is a humor [disposition] that make the men active, earnest, full of alacrity and stirring, if it not be stopped. But, if it be stopped, and cannot have his way, it becometh adust [burned up], and thereby malign and venomous. So ambitious men, if they find the way open for their rising, and still get forward, they are rather busy than dangerous; but, if they be checked for their desires, they become secretly discontent, and look upon men and matters, with an evil eye; and are best pleased when things go backwards; which is the worst property, in a servant of a prince or the state.[12]

Having explained the nature of ambitious men, Francis Bacon concludes that ultimately the greatest good is done by those who are "more sensible of duty than of rising."[13] In other words, by those who can rise above their self-interest. However, it is not easy for human beings to break away from the pull of "I, me and mine." Consequently, nations, societies and organizations that value leadership use various techniques to create environments in which leaders can rise above their self-interest and sublimate their personal ambitions (which are quite natural in a person) to higher ideals.

43

Organizational Culture Designed to Promote Selflessness

Organizational culture is the management name for esprit de corps in the armed forces. Esprit de corps has been defined as "regard for the honor and interest of the body one belongs to."[14] The aim of esprit de corps is that everyone in an organization be imbued with a feeling that "no sacrifice is big enough to uphold its [the organization's] honor and good name."[15] Most Japanese executives, and indeed many others round the globe, feel that their primary role is to create such an organizational culture. But how is it that the Japanese have succeeded so well in their enterprises while examples of success elsewhere are rather rare (we shall see one of these rare examples in the culture that prevailed in the worldwide chain of Hard Rock Cafes).

To understand the Japanese miracle, we have to understand the culture of samurai and the spirit of bushido. Both are a tradition of practicing human values that helps a Japanese rise far above self-interest.

In describing the cultural heritage of Japan, *samurai* is the word used to refer to a Japanese warrior who adopted a lifestyle that lauded bravery, honor and loyalty to one's shogun (lord) as more important than life itself. A samurai was trained in, among other skills, developing tenacious willpower by fasting and running barefoot on snow. It helped to instill in him the spirit of Bushido. *Bushido* means the "way of the warrior." It was a code of behavior stressing loyalty, courage and duty. The samurai was groomed "to be always ready and for sacrifice." In the ancient books of Japan, Bushido has been described as "the way of dying." The overall training of a samurai was twofold—the pen and the sword. This meant "leadership and arts plus swordsmanship and strategy."

It is worth noting that during World War II Japanese soldiers were fully imbued with Bushido. During six years of that war, over a million soldiers of all nationalities were captured as prisoners of war. Among them, the Japanese were just a few hundred. For a Japanese soldier, it was far more honorable to die, even by *seppuku* (slashing the stomach with a small sword) than to face the stigma and dishonor of surviving as a prisoner. In addition, the spiritual heritage of Japan has instilled in the people the habit of humility and hard work.

Japan was defeated in World War II. It has hardly any natural resources. The population of Japan is less than that of the state of California in the USA or Bihar in India. And yet it has become the most powerful economic nation in the world. How?

The Japanese political, industrial and enterprise shoguns (leaders) rising from the ashes of their defeat were able to develop industrial samurais and instill in them the spirit of economic Bushido. No sacrifice was big enough to make Japan a "number one" economic country. It is indeed a transparent example of what leaders can achieve if their foundation is firmly based on duty, sacrifice, humility and hard work and if they are inspired by a vision far higher than themselves.

Armed forces round the world have known that leadership is the biggest single factor in determining the fortunes of war. They adopt many a measure to inculcate selflessness among their officers. Some examples merit attention.

In most countries of the British Commonwealth, when a young potential officer goes to a military academy for training, he is designated as a gentleman cadet. He is not referred to as a probationer or an officer trainee or an officer cadet. There is a significant purpose in this practice. He is reminded repeatedly that he will make a good officer if he is first of all a gentleman. And the description of a gentleman is explained to him (see the description of a man of character earlier in this chapter). It is a well-tried-out technique of autosuggestion that you can transform the character of a person by repeatedly suggesting to him or her a pattern: "what you think, so you become." The technique does have an influence.

Many armed forces in the world have a "honor code" system during three or four years of the training period for their officers. The purpose of the system is to remove three infirmities from a person's character. The system demands that "you will not steal, lie or cheat." If you do, then you are expected to own it and accept a corrective punishment. If you know about another person breaking any of these rules, you are expected to report it.

Similarly, most armed forces in the world give their officers a lifelong credo to live by during service. For example, U.S. Army officers carry from their training academy at West Point the credo "Duty, Honor, Country" to guide them through their career. The interest of these three comes before self-interest.

The Indian Army credo for its officers is very explicit. It commits them to keep their self-interest as the very last item of what they are expected to do:

> The Safety, Honor and Welfare of the country come first, always and every time.
>
> The Honor, Welfare and Comfort of the men you command come next.
>
> Your own Ease, Comfort and Safety come last, always and every time.

The ideal in the Indian Army credo is that the country comes first, your men next and yourself last—particularly, your safety comes the very last! It has inspired officers to rise to great heights of self-sacrifice in many a battle fought by the Indian Army all over the world. Let us look at the example of one Major Prithi Chand, who earned the Maha Vir Chakra (Medal for Exceptional

Gallantry). Almost single-handedly, he saved Ladakh (an extension of the Tibetan plateau forming a huge district of the state of Jammu and Kashmir in India) from being captured by Pakistan during 1947-48 war between India and Pakistan.

Major Prithi Chand Saves Ladakh

This is the story of a man who was inspired by an ideal—an example of selflessness of one leader who raised the vision of people all around him to achieve the impossible.

Prithi Chand was a scion of the ruling family of Lahul, a small principality tucked into the Himalayas, to the north of Kulu and Manali. It borders on Ladakh.

In 1936, when Prithi Chand was about to finish his studies, the family guru visited him. He came from his Buddhist monastery in Ladakh. The guru was ailing and said that the visit would be his last one. One evening he looked straight into the eyes of Prithi Chand and asked him to promise him something. Prithi Chand readily offered to do whatever the guru wanted. "Protect my monastery when it is in danger." Not knowing what it meant, Prithi Chand promised to do so.

On the eve of World War II, Prithi Chand joined the Indian Army as an officer. The war years rolled by. In 1947, India won her independence and was divided into two countries—India and Pakistan. Jammu and Kashmir was a princely state; the king had the right to join India or Pakistan. To force the issue, Pakistan invaded Jammu and Kashmir in October 1947. To survive the invasion, the king acceded to India and asked for military help. The Indian Army units were flown in to stem the attack.

It was December 1947 when Major Prithi Chand's battalion arrived in the Kashmir valley. Soon thereafter, the Himalayas received a heavy snowfall, and the only route leading to Ladakh across the Himalayas at Zojila pass was blocked for the duration of the winter.

One of the thrusts of the Pakistani invasion was along the Indus River towards Leh, the capital of Ladakh. The Indus River here is on the northern side of the Himalayas and flows from Tibet in the east towards west. In the severe wintry conditions, the invading column was making slow progress against resistance being put up by a small force belonging to the state of Jammu and Kashmir.

The Ladakhi community in Srinagar, the capital of Kashmir, started getting news of the imminent fall of Ladakh. During the long winter ahead, it was only a matter of time before the invaders would reach and capture Leh. On a tenuous radio link the news started coming in that people were packing up their belongings to send them away to Tibet along with their women and children. Major Prithi Chand was getting all this news through a Ladakhi classmate, who was a civil engineer in Srinagar.

One night Major Prithi Chand had a brief dream. His guru appeared before him and told him to fulfill his promise. Prithi Chand woke up with a start. What promise? He had completely forgotten the incident of 1936. Slowly the memory came back.

Prithi Chand got up, put on his uniform and set to work. He had gotten clear-cut ideal to save Ladakh, to protect the monastery of his guru. His mission was more important than his life.

The senior military commanders felt that Prithi Chand had gone mad when he suggested that an operation should be mounted to protect Ladakh. There was no way Ladakh could be saved. The route had closed down for the winter. And, in any case, they had no force that could be diverted from the difficult task of protecting the Kashmir valley.

Prithi Chand was not discouraged. He knocked at every door—military as well as political. He even persuaded the Ladakhi community to send telegrams to the prime minister of India in Delhi.

Finally, military authorities relented and approved a plan prepared by Prithi Chand. Privately, they were of the opinion that it was a most scatterbrained idea. But they agreed to it to get Prithi Chand off their backs! The plan was that Major Prithi Chand, along with 13 volunteers from his battalion and his civil engineer friend, would cross the snowbound Himalayas. They would carry about 200 rifles and some ammunition on porters. On reaching Ladakh, Prithi Chand would raise a guerrilla force from the local youth and train them. They would then delay the Pakistani invading columns. Simultaneously, the civil engineer would prepare an airfield at Leh for the military aircraft—Dakotas. Once the airfield was ready, reinforcements would be flown into Ladakh.

The Indian military commanders were quite willing to write off the major, 13 soldiers and some arms to remove the nuisance that Major Prithi Chand had become!

The story of Major Prithi Chand is one of the great sagas of the arms profession. It needs a full book to narrate his adventures. But, in a nutshell, he did cross the Himalayas in midwinter, escape an avalanche, reach Ladakh and raise a guerrilla force. He did hold the Pakistani invaders at bay for sixty days, get the airfield ready at Leh, and pester the military authorities to honor their promise to fly in reinforcements just in time to prevent the fall of Leh! He was awarded a Maha Vir Chakra, but his greater reward was the fulfillment of an ideal.

Selflessness based on an ideal or a vision is the real foundation of leadership. It inspires a leader, and also those he leads, to achieve the impossible. Let us now look at an example of what it does in the mundane world of business.

Hard Rock Cafes

The Hard Rock Cafes form a chain of restaurants spanning almost the whole world. How did a young man named Isaac Tigrett, hardly out of his teens, set up this miniempire. He was able to do it because he is the living model of selflessness based on an ideal, as depicted in figure 3.2. His presence makes a physical impact of peace, love and joy.

Isaac is the scion of a wealthy family. He was raised in Jackson, Tennessee, a town that is 90 percent black. The town was an example of segregation of Whites and Blacks at its worst. This injustice deeply hurt the loving heart of young Isaac Tigrett. And then, a few years later, in 1964, the Civil Rights Act was passed in the USA, ending segregation and guaranteeing equality to all. Overnight, discriminatory signboards saying Whites Only or Blacks Not Allowed were taken down. This example of man-made division between people, and then its almost complete removal overnight, left an indelible imprint on Isaac's mind—all men are, in reality, equal. He was still in his teens when his parents divorced. Isaac gave up his studies and moved with his father to England. Instead of going to an academic institution, he joined the "university of life" and started working in one of his father's factories. He was appalled by the working conditions in the factory. But what hurt him more deeply was the class division in England. It was the Jackson segregation in another form. The management had absolutely no interaction with the workers. Without any formal signboards, the upper classes and lower classes had their separate eating places, clubs and pubs. Incensed by the blatant injustice of it all, Isaac led a strike of the workers against the management of his father's factory!

Slowly Isaac made up his mind to break the segregation in the British society. What a lofty ideal for humanity. But how?

In the environments of the 1960s, when youth were talking a lot about love, Isaac thought of a novel idea. He decided to set up in London—the snootiest city in the world—a completely classless restaurant where a baker and banker could sit and eat at the same table.

Isaac, hardly out of his teens, flew to the USA. Using his family name and stature he borrowed $60,000 from his hometown banker, enough to rent space and set up his restaurant in the snootiest neighborhood of London—Mayfair.

In keeping with the craze for rock music during the 1960s, he named his restaurant the Hard Rock Cafe. The spirit of the restaurant would be the friendly informality of the Southern states in the USA. Under it all lay the inflexible determination of its leader—Isaac Tigrett—to "break the system."' He converted his ideal into action for the "unity of man."

With its courteous and loving service, the cafe was an instant hit. Customers from all strata of society—lawyers, bankers, cab drivers, cockneys from the newspaper stands, and blue- and white-collar workers—waited patiently for their turn to get a table.

Working completely by instinct, but working very hard with common sense and caring for people, Isaac evolved the culture of the Hard Rock Cafe. The workers were bound together by immense pride in their venture. Hard Rock Cafe people became a family who were prepared for any sacrifice for the honor and good name of their restaurant.

Isaac had workers from all cultures in his "rainbow collection" ("they spoke as many as twenty-five native languages"). He welded them together by regularly holding family meetings of the entire staff. He asked them to give him their experience and ideas to make the venture a success. The meetings were uproarious. Ideas about "kindness, about quality through politeness, and about our themes: classlessness and aggressive American friendliness" [16] were used to train the workers. Isaac "wanted the place to exude love." [17]

The motto of the cafe, "Love All, Serve All", was displayed prominently in bold brass letters. Along with it was also a beautiful large photograph of Isaac Tigrett's spiritual mentor—Sathya Sai Baba. There is little doubt that Isaac was translating the great teaching of his mentor into action:

> there is only one nation, the nation of humanity;
> there is only one religion, the religion of love;
> there is only one language, the language of the heart;
> there is only one God and he is omnipresent.

Instinctively Isaac made his workers the main instruments of his business. He "instituted the first-ever profit-sharing plan in a restaurant business in England." [18] He ensured that the scoring system for this sharing included due weightage for "friendliness, helpfulness, and fitting into the family." [19] Women were paid the same wage as men, contrary to the then prevailing practice of paying them only half! Workers could phone Isaac directly.

Employment in the chain of Hard Rock Cafes, which soon spread all over the world, became a place of transformation for people. "I could hire those no one else would take, and in six or seven months they would be new people .... Here they were loved, and they loved back in return." [20]

Isaac loved his customers just as much as his workers. When the lines became very long, they were taken care of even as they waited. Umbrellas were distributed if it rained, iced tea when it was hot, and hot cocoa or soup when it was freezing cold. People loved it. Business boomed. Isaac diversified to a few selected items of garments stamped with "Love All, Serve All."

At about the age of 40, Isaac sold off the world chain of Hard Rock ventures for a fabulous price of U.S. $107 million. He put the bulk of this money in a charitable trust named the Rama Foundation and has now moved on to other pastures.

What has Isaac achieved by being a man of character, as described in this chapter, or by being the embodiment of selflessness, as depicted in figure 3.2? Money? But that is the least of his concerns. His great achievement is the vast number of people he has influenced to practice human values. And he has transformed them with the irresistible force of his personal example. It is leaders like Isaac Tigrett who will help humanity to move towards its final destination:

Unity of Man, Global Economy and Earth Citizenship.

It is appropriate to end the discussion in this chapter on selflessness (unselfishness, self-sacrifice or whatever) with the views of three great teachers:

> Whosoever wishes to be the first among you shall be your servant.   —Jesus Christ

> A "sardar" [leader] must be a "sirdar" [a person ready to lay down his or her head]. —Swami Vivekananda

> As long you are clouded over with this possessive attitude, thinking only of yourself, your family, your people and your things, you can be certain that sooner or later you will be cast into sorrow. You must travel from the stage of identifying yourself with "I" and "mine" to the higher stage where you are constantly identifying yourself with "we" and "ours." From

selfishness you must gradually travel to selflessness, from bondage to liberation.　　　—Sathya Sai Baba

Note for Teachers

1. "The Foundation of Leadership" is the most important chapter of the book. Educational systems all over the world are currently placing a major emphasis on self-interest of students. Consequently, the entire outlook of youth is focused on career goals—the status and wealth that they will generate with the help of their learning. If teachers are to make selflessness acceptable as the foundation for leadership, it will require all their skill, conviction and personal example. Not only that. As examined in chapter 1, selflessness *thyaga* is also the only way to the spiritual goal of life and, as we shall see later, the real source of happiness (see chapter 7).

2. The description of a man of character by Taya Zinkin paraphrases human values in various aspects of our behavior. Students enjoy and also learn by relating each sentence of the description to the value enshrined in it. Also ask them to improve on the description if they can. Such an assignment makes a lasting impact on an individual.

3. Encourage students to identify acts of selfishness and selflessness in their own behavior. After one or two individuals set the ball rolling, this exercise makes honest introspection virtually a competitive avalanche. In this discussion, we realize that our motives for doing things decide whether our action is selfless or selfish.

4. Many individuals do not believe in God. Encourage them to discuss what 'conscience' or 'inner voice' means. As long as they understand that there is some force inside us that helps us to judge what is right and wrong, or what is good and bad, then labels do not matter.

5. The life of General Matthew Ridgway is an inspiring story. Students should be encouraged to read whatever is available about his life and career. They should then judge why he has included what he has in his descriptions of a man of character. Also, encourage them to find other real-life stories, like those of Major Prithi Chand and Isaac Tigrett.

4

To Be: Universal Inner Structure of Good Leaders: Essential Qualities

A very large number of qualities determine the character of a person. Scores of qualities have been listed in the literature on leadership. However, the core qualities that are really important and are invariably found in the character of all outstanding leaders are shown in "Universal Inner Structure of Good Leaders," figure 3.1 and the linked figure explaining the foundation of leadership at 3.2. We have discussed the foundation quality of the character of a good leader—selflessness—in chapter 3. We shall discuss in this chapter the other three qualities of character essential in a good leader. These are:

- Courage

- Willpower

- Initiative

Courage

Courage is the most admired human virtue in all societies; to be courageous is to be like a lion.

The most important act of courage for a leader is to make decisions. No action can start unless a decision is made. To make a decision means being accountable for success or failure; that is why a large number of people procrastinate. It is important that decisions are made with care and after fully weighing the pros and cons of the available options. But, even after that, the best option is seldom crystal clear. Most decisions have to be made in an atmosphere of uncertainty about the outcome. In the military, this uncertainty is called the fog of war. We have to remember that nothing moves or happens without a decision. That is why it is said that a bad decision is better than no decision at all.

There are many other facets of courage that are important. For example:

- One who is courageous will not lie; cowardice makes a person hide the truth.

- It is an expression of courage to demand high standards of performance even at the cost of being unpopular.

- To punish requires courage. Quite often, compassion is made an alibi for lack of courage. Mistakes and acts of omission or commission have a habit of snowballing if these are not promptly corrected. All punishment, however, should be administered in the spirit with which a good mother uses the rod—to improve.

- It takes courage to say no to an act that is unethical.

A leader needs both physical and moral courage. The total span of moral courage that enables a person to draw many others to him or her in any age is beautifully described in the following words:

Quiet resolution;
The hardihood to take risks;
The will to take full responsibility for decisions;
The readiness to share its rewards with subordinates;
An equal readiness to take the blame when things go adversely;
The nerve to survive storm and disappointment, and to face each new day with the score sheet wiped clean, neither

dwelling on one's success, nor accepting discouragement from one's failures.[1]

Again, it is courage that gives distinctive direction to the entire approach of a leader's work. Peter Drucker, the doyen of management science, advises that:

> Courage rather than analysis dictates the truly important rules for identifying priorities. Pick the future as against the past; focus on opportunities, rather than on problems; choose your own direction, rather than climb the bandwagon, and aim high. Aim that will make a difference rather than something safe and easy to do.[2]

Aiming high means raising the vision above "what is good for me," to an ideal that will benefit many.

Finally, the most potent source of courage, both physical and moral, lies in the ancient Indian truth that soul (*atma*) does not die; indeed, it is eternal and indestructible. This truth forms the central message of the *Bhagavad Gita*. This knowledge makes a person *nirbhaya*, meaning "fearless." And those who put in the necessary effort to experience this truth become *abhaya*, meaning "one who knows no fear at all." And this brings us to the key question: How can we experience this truth? The answer lies in having the "willpower" to make the necessary effort.

Willpower

Willpower to persist is a quality present in all outstanding leaders. "Willpower is the king of all faculties—it is the source of all other faculties."[3]

In the implementation of any plan, program or project, hundreds of difficulties arise. Failures occur when people have to execute the plan. Sometimes, these failures are due to natural causes; at other times, to insufficient resources; or to the frailties of human nature. A good leader must have the willpower (call it determination, perseverance, tenacity or whatever) to persist in spite of setbacks and difficulties that may arise.

The whole purpose of this book is to enthuse the reader, to develop his or her leadership potential to the maximum. To succeed in this endeavor, willpower is the most crucial faculty. The experience of research and experiments since 1979 indicates that almost all of us are anxious to improve ourselves. Unfortunately, those of us who stay the course to change and transform our habits of thought, word and action represent less than 15 percent of the population. Most of us lack the necessary willpower to do so. That is the reason this quality has been designated as the king of all faculties.

"Try, Try, again" is an age old advice based on the famous poem about Robert the Bruce. The value of dogged perseverance was once articulated in a most dramatic manner by Sir Winston Churchill, who was the prime minister of the United Kingdom during World War II. He came out of the war as one of the tallest leaders in the world. He was invited to be the guest of honor at the celebration of the 150th anniversary of his school. He was also requested to deliver the keynote address to inspire the students to follow his example and become outstanding leaders in their own right. Churchill accepted the invitation. All segments of society had great expectations about hearing views on his leadership.

On the appointed day, the hall where the function was being held was overflowing with people. The media and the scholars had turned up in strength. Everyone was looking forward to Sir Winston's revealing the secrets of his leadership. After the usual courtesies, Churchill was invited to deliver his keynote address. He got up from his chair, walked slowly to the podium, took out small rectangular glasses, and put them on. He then took out a small piece of paper, placed it on the podium, and peered over his glasses at the audience. There was pin-drop silence. He then delivered his address:

NEVER,
NEVER,
NEVER,
NEVER,
GIVE UP.

Having roared these five words, he ambled back to his seat. There was a bewildered hush for a long time. However, his great message soon sank home. People stood up and gave him a long and thunderous ovation.

In just five words Churchill had distilled the great secret of his leadership and success. In his checkered life, he had seen many ups and downs, but he never lost heart. When the time came, he was ready to lead his nation from almost total defeat to final victory in the greatest and the bloodiest war yet fought in human history.

Another example that illustrates the value of willpower is its contribution to the success story of the worldwide fast food chain McDonald's in the USA. The company attributes its excellence to the determination of everyone in the chain to serve customers fresh, fast and clean food with alacrity and dispatch. To ensure that the needed determination does not lose vigor, a step has been adopted. The following *poster* is prominently displayed in the office of each and every manager of the enterprise:

DETERMINATION

NOTHING IN THE WORLD CAN TAKE THE
PLACE OF PERSISTENCE:

TALENT WILL NOT: NOTHING IS MORE
COMMON THAN UNSUCCESSFUL MEN WITH
GREAT TALENT.

GENIUS WILL NOT: UNREWARDED GENIUS IS
ALMOST A PROVERB.

EDUCATION WILL NOT: THE WORLD IS FULL
OF EDUCATED DERELICTS.

PERSISTENCE, DETERMINATION ALONE ARE
OMNIPOTENT.

We shall see in chapter 7 how anyone who has the necessary willpower can become the master of his or her destiny. This quality is the key to self-development. If it is strengthened and reinforced, then transforming our character becomes an achievable goal. Transforming means getting rid of our bad habits—our infirmities—which are embedded in lust, anger, attachment, greed, egotism and jealousy and then imbibing or reinforcing the qualities that form part of the universal inner structure of good leaders, as explained in figures 3.1 and 3.2. The experience of thousands of years of Indian spiritual practices designed to transform individuals has been articulated thus:

> For him who has struggled with external tendencies
> and conquered them, the internal tendencies become
> easily controllable.[4]

Consequently, self-denial of desires and physical needs has been harnessed in the following ways to develop willpower:

- Fasting has been used to reinforce willpower in all cultures. In Islam, fasting (*rozas*) for 30 days during the month of Ramadan is a well-established technique for purifying the mind and strengthening willpower. The Japanese samurais combined fasting with running barefoot on snow for the same purpose. A water fast of 40 days in Indian spiritual

61

practice is perhaps the most rigorous means towards the same end.

- Revolutionaries have used the technique of placing their hand on a burning candle for a long time without flinching. This practice steels the mind.

- Giving up sugar or salt for a fixed period serves the same purpose.

- A bath in ice cold water during winter helps.

- Limiting sleep to say 6½ hours per day, instead of 8 hours, serves the same purpose. In addition, it also gives nearly 450 hours of extra time per year for studies or other productive work.

- Giving up addiction to bad habits like drinking, smoking, chewing pan, inhaling snuff, watching TV far too long, and so on also strengthens willpower.

- Long-distance endurance running, maybe three times a week, not only strengthens willpower but also adds to good health.

While building our willpower to persevere, it is good to remember the well-known words of Henry Wadsworth Longfellow:

> The heights by great men reached and kept, were not attained by sudden flight. But they, while their companions slept, were toiling upwards in the night.

A few words of caution are appropriate when we talk of willpower. Plain obstinacy should not be mistaken for willpower. Obstinacy is usually the product of vanity or egotism or sheer ignorance. The line between obstinacy and willpower is very thin. A leader who has the flexibility and initiative to change the method of implementing a plan without forsaking its purpose has the right touch. "There is always the danger that determination becomes plain obstinacy; flexibility mere vacillation. If you can hold in yourself the balance between these two—strength of will and flexibility of mind—you will be well on the road to being leader in a big way."[5]

When the source of willpower is our conscience (the inner voice), it helps us persist on the right course. However, when the source is our egotism, then it invariably ends up in obstinacy. Many a dictator of immense willpower linked to egotism turned megalomaniac and brought great suffering to his people—Hitler and Stalin are two examples.

Basically, it is initiative that prompts a leader when to change his method without sacrificing the goal. Consequently, initiative is the third virtue that is universal in all outstanding leaders.

Initiative

Effective leaders are always two jumps ahead of events. They do this by intelligent anticipation, based on a sound information system that overcomes difficulties and obstacles as these crop up. Such leaders are also on the lookout for openings and opportunities to exploit for the furtherance of their task. All these abilities are signs of initiative. In a nutshell, people of initiative are self-starters, and that makes them dynamic.

On the contrary, people without initiative hang around waiting for things to happen. They are afraid to stick their neck out. "No one told me," "I was not ordered," "I did not know," and so on are the utterances of executives who lack initiative. One with initiative makes things happen.

Fear of making a mistake curbs initiative. Consequently, mutual confidence and trust accompanied by delegation of authority and responsibility create an environment in which initiative blooms the most. It is important that a senior leader create such an environment in the sphere of his responsibility. It is in such an environment that we learn that "to err is not human."[6]

If we use our discrimination properly, then chances of making a mistake become less. And even if a mistake is made, it is corrected promptly—more as a process of learning than as a retribution. Consequently, initiative blooms.

Initiative can be developed by the habit of forethought. A leader should take some quiet time to reflect on the chosen course of action, to visualize the likely snags and difficulties that can arise. He would then be mentally prepared if some of the anticipated problems do crop up, and be able to modify or adopt an alternative course of action with dispatch and vigor.

Perhaps, the biggest source of initiative is a habit that fixes the vision of a person far above his or her job. We should start every day by asking ourselves a question: "What can I do this day to contribute to the excellence of my organization?"[7]

The question is not related merely to one's job; that would limit the sights to efficiency. It should pertain to the organization as a whole. Such a question raises our own vision as well as that of those around us. This attitude is the fountainhead of initiative. And a leader with this habit, in the long run, equips himself or herself for shouldering higher responsibilities.

To appreciate that almost every component essential to becoming a good and effective leader is contained in the universal inner structure of good leaders, an exercise is useful.

Exercise 4.1: Attributes of Successful Leaders

In England, a survey was undertaken among a cross section of the most successful chief executives of enterprises to determine the attributes that helped them rise to the top. The 25 attributes listed below in a jumbled order emerged as the most important.

You may arrange these attributes in the order of merit that you consider appropriate for reaching the top. Also, for each attribute write the component of the universal inner structure of good leaders (explained in figures 3.1 and 3.2) that you consider its source.

After you have done the exercise, you can see the actual order of merit that emerged from the ground survey. The actual order, as well as the source of each attribute in the universal inner structure of good leaders, is shown in table 4.1.

Ambition

Willingness to work hard

Enterprise

Astuteness

Ability to "stick to it"

Capacity for lucid writing

Imagination

Ability to spot opportunities

Curiosity

Understanding others

Skill with numbers

Capacity for abstract thought

Willingness to work long hours

Integrity

Ability to administer efficiently

Enthusiasm

Capacity to speak lucidly

Single-mindedness

Willingness to take risks

Leadership

Ability to make decisions

Analytical ability

Ability to meet unpleasant situations

Open-mindedness

Ability to adapt quickly to change

Table 4.1: Ranking of Attributes by Successful Chief Executives in England

	Attribute	Source of the Attribute in Universal Inner Structure of Good Leaders
1.	Ability to make decisions	Courage
2.	Leadership	Universal inner structure of good leaders
3.	Integrity	Selflessness, right conduct
4.	Enthusiasm	Vision and knowledge
5.	Imagination	Ideal/vision and knowledge of job
6.	Willingness to work hard	Willpower
7.	Analytical ability	Knowledge of job and self
8.	Understanding others	Dealing with people
9.	Ability to spot opportunities	Initiative
10.	Ability to meet unpleasant situations	Courage
11.	Ability to adapt quickly change	Initiative and knowing the job
12.	Willingness to take risks	Courage
13.	Enterprise	Initiative

Table 4.1 (Continued)

Attribute	Source of the Attribute in Universal Inner Structure of Good Leaders
14. Capacity to speak lucidly	Communication skill in dealing with people
15. Astuteness	Knowledge
16. Ability to administer efficiently	Knowledge of job Dealing with people
17. Open-mindedness	Selflessness
18. Ability to stick to it	Willpower
19. Willingness to work long hours	Willpower
20. Ambitions	Ideal or vision
21. Single-mindedness	Willpower
22. Capacity for lucid writing	Communication skill in dealing with people
23. Curiosity	Initiative and knowing the job
24. Skill with numbers	Knowledge of the job
25. Capacity for abstract thought	Selflessness based on vision.

Note for Teachers

1. Students should be encouraged to gather and write real-life stories of courage, willpower and initiative—particularly among their peers.

2. To develop willpower is a very exciting undertaking. It's best to start with simple targets. Each target achieved enthuses us to greater effort. This action program should run for months.

3. After doing the exercise, students may be asked to decide which of the three source qualities—courage, willpower or initiative—comes out on top.

5

To Be: Universal Inner Structure of Good Leaders: Knowledge of Job and Self

Knowledge is an important component of the universal inner structure of good leaders and has three subdivisions, as shown in figure 3.1:

- Knowledge of the job

- Knowledge of self

- Capability of dealing with people

Capability of dealing with people includes essential knowledge about human nature. It also encompasses the entire strength of the rest of the structure. This combined force allows a leader to deal with people in such a way that they give their best, no matter what the circumstances are. We shall discuss this capability in chapter 6.

The real value of knowledge lies in what a leader learns through his or her own efforts. A leader's direct experience in a chosen field of work cannot truly be replaced by any other device. Yet learning from the experience of other people has been the very hallmark of all outstanding leaders. Learning is a lifelong and continuous process. The reading habit is the biggest single factor that contributes towards indirect experience. "The great value of indirect experience lies in the greater variety and spread of knowledge. History is a universal experience not of another, but of many others."[1] A survey in the USA shows that most of the chief executives read an average of 19 books a year, including 10 nonfiction works. The library is a very potent source of information on strengthening leadership.

Knowledge of the Job

Knowledge of the field of work they have chosen gives leaders great strength. Knowledge is power is a well-known maxim. It is, indeed, a fact that "a group of people can often be dominated by one person who sees most clearly."[2] Knowledge of the total system in a chosen field and the internal and external environments of the organization are also necessary for getting things done.

Leaders develop best if their field of work is in keeping with their aptitude and liking. Assuming that the field is chosen well, leaders should widen their knowledge and technical competence in their job. In the fast-changing world of technology, updating knowledge is essential. This helps leaders acquire the flexibility needed for responding to changes and the necessary confidence to deal with people.

Learning from the knowledge and experience of others should be cultivated by leaders early in life. "Wisdom begins at a point of understanding that there is nothing shameful about ignorance."[3] An inquisitive and open mind and acceptance of informed criticism are essential for the enrichment and growth of knowledge.

The ultimate goal of knowledge in a leader's chosen field of work is to develop intuition—at times also referred to as the sixth sense. It is somewhat similar to the clinical sense of a competent medical practitioner. Intuition has been defined as "the power of mind by which it immediately perceives the truth of things without reasoning or analysis." It is distilled experience and the result of years of learning every aspect of one's chosen field of work. Acquiring knowledge with common sense is the royal road to intuition. Common sense is the ability to sweep aside trivial concerns and get to the core of what really matters.

70

That which deals with one of the more difficult fields of knowledge is understanding our own nature, our weaknesses and strengths.

Knowledge of Self

A good leader must understand his or her own character. This is absolutely vital. Leadership is the interaction between the leader and the led. A good leader must know and understand both parties.

The human tragedy is such that each of us feels that we are the epitome of perfection, and so we refuse to look at ourself as in a mirror.

There is a sound and noble core in every person. However, unfortunately, it gets coated with layers of egotism, desire, greed, anger and jealousy of varying thickness. Deeply involved in these layers, we refuse even to realize that we may have some shortcomings. We blame others for being "let down," "deceived," and so on. Let us look at the well-known example of two brothers to understand this point.

Two brothers in an affluent family had grown up in the same town. They had a common heritage and had grown up in exactly the same environments. However, by the time they finished college, each had a totally different nature and temperament. One day the elder brother was crossing the family living room barefooted. Around the middle of the room, he ran into a metallic tumbler left by a child. Not having seen it, he hit it with force that caused him immense pain. He started to howl and shout, "I know someone deliberately placed the tumbler in my way so that I would get hurt. Everyone in this house is against me. They are jealous of me and want to injure me. Why must people be so mean?" And on and on he went. On hearing all the ruckus, the younger brother ran into the room and hit the very same tumbler with greater force than his brother. It nearly fractured his big toe. But his reaction was different. All he said was "I must be blind to run into such a big glass. I must be more careful."

In this example, the elder brother would need a good deal of reprogramming (in computer language) of his nature even to have the rudimentary potential for leadership. The younger brother, on the other hand, is sound material for growth. Those who understand their own character are never afflicted by self-created doubts that adversely affect their ability to deal with other people.

Self-knowledge is also a step towards understanding others, which is essential for harmonious interpersonal relationships. Without self-knowledge in a group, many covert behaviors that delay, oppose and even sabotage the work can slowly develop. A very useful test that helps us understand our attitude towards others has been devised by Professor William Schutz. The Fundamental Interpersonal Relation Orientation of Behavior (FIROB) test focuses on the underlying reality of our character in three areas of interpersonal behavior:

- Desire to be social and expectation that others will be likewise

- Desire to control and expectation that others will control us

- Desire to love and expectation that love will come from others

As a broad rule, birds of opposite feather get on well with one another! For example, a person who wants to control others will get on well with a person who wants to be controlled. On the other hand, there is likely to be conflict if the controller is dealing with a person who also wants to control.

It is useful to take this test to understand how we are likely to react to other people. This requires the assistance of a counsellor who has experience in interpreting the test.

However, if we understand that knowing our own strengths and weaknesses is essential for self-development, then there is quite a bit that we can do ourselves. Our inability to look at ourselves with clinical detachment puts us "on a self-deceiving, self-justifying path often involving rationalization (rational lies) to self and others."[4] In the bargain, we injure ourselves deeply and struggle through life, blaming others.

The best method of knowing ourself is to look at ourself in deep silence and ask questions about ourself. Our conscience will invariably give us the right answers. If we examine the motives behind our thoughts, words and actions, then we start understanding ourselves. One way to do this is to ask questions related to the universal inner structure of good leaders. For example:

- Are my thoughts, words and actions always pure? Was there an occasion recently when it was not so?

- Can I be considered a person of integrity—acting according to what is expected of me in my position?

- Am I honest? Was there an occasion recently when I lied, cheated or stole?

- Am I loyal? Or does my loyalty change to suit my self-interest?

- Do I have faith in God? Or do I remember him only when in trouble?

- Is my motive in saying and doing things my self-interest? Or do I have an ideal higher than I, me and myself?

- Do I have the courage to make decisions, knowing that these can turn out to be wrong? Or do I procrastinate or try to involve my superior in making decisions?

- Do I have the patience and persistence to apply myself to a task till it is successfully completed? Or do I give up when faced with difficulties, or out of sheer laziness?

- Do I take initiative? Or do I like to drift along?

- Do I have the knowledge, skill and capability to achieve excellence in my work? Have I updated my knowledge?

- Can I get people to respond positively to accomplish whatever has to be done?

- Do I know my own strengths and weaknesses? Or do I believe that I am perfect, but that people are jealous of me and won't cooperate with me?

Many other instruments have been developed to permit us to evaluate our own potential. Three such instruments in the form of simple exercises are included here.

While doing self-assessment, some of the common words mean different things to different people. It is, therefore, useful to clearly define some of these words:

Purity—no duplicity, insincerity or hypocrisy in our thought, word and deed

Integrity—uprightness, soundness, honesty; in Sanskrit, closest to *dharma*, which means "right conduct"

Loyalty—Truthfulness; faithfulness to duty, love or obligation, or in allegiance to the government or country

Honesty—being fair and righteous in speech and act; not lying, cheating or stealing

Holistic (from holism)—the tendency in nature to form wholes that are more than the sum of the parts by ordered grouping

Checklist and Questions For Leadership Qualities

Exercise 5.1, "Do You Have Some Basic Leadership Potential?," helps us determine whether we have the rudimentary aptitude for leadership. The value of this exercise depends on the honesty and detachment with which we judge ourselves. It has three parts. Part I, a checklist, deals with the five key characteristics required in the field of work we are interested or involved in. Part II is a self-appraisal of whether we are introverted. Part III deals with other qualities that indicate our basic potential for leadership. The higher the proportion of yes answers in this part, the higher the potential.

Self-Appraisal

Exercise 5.2, "Self-Appraisal," has two parts. Part I gives us an opportunity to judge ourselves and to contrast our self-image with the way we would prefer to be. It also provides us with an opportunity to obtain the judgment of another person whom we trust and feel would give us honest and objective feedback. Part II gives us an opportunity to determine where we stand between being effective and ineffective as leaders. Detailed instructions are given on how to answer questions in the exercise. The usefulness of the exercise depends on the honesty and detachment with which we judge ourselves. When we request a friend to give us feedback, then we have to be careful on one count. Our friend should grade us without seeing our self-appraisal. Similarly, we should grade ourselves without seeing the appraisal by our friend. Then only will we get an objective picture.

Exercise 5.1: Do you have some basic leadership potential?[5]

Part I: Checklist

List the five key qualities that are expected in the field of work you're interested in. Then rate yourself:

	Good	**Average**	**Weak**
1.			
2.			
3.			
4.			
15.			

Part II

Circle the number where you would place yourself on the continuum.

Very Introverted   Very Extroverted
     5   4 3 2 1 2 3 4   5

Leaders tend to be slightly more extroverted than introverted on this scale; they are a mixture of both.

Part III

	Yes	No
1. Have you shown yourself to be a responsible person?	☐	☐
2. Do you like the responsibility as well the rewards of leadership?	☐	☐

3. Are you self-sufficient enough to withstand unpopularity or criticism or indifference from others, and to work effectively with others without constant supervision? ☐ ☐

4. Are you an active and socially participative person? ☐ ☐

5. Can you control your emotions and moods, or do they control you? ☐ ☐

6. Have you any evidence to suppose that other people think of you as essentially a warm person? ☐ ☐

7. Can you give instances over the past three months where you have been deliberately dishonest, or less than straight, with people you are associated with? Are you noted for your enthusiasm at work? ☐ ☐

8. Has anyone used the word integrity in relation to you? ☐ ☐

Exercise 5.2: Self-Appraisal[6]

This exercise gives you the opportunity to appraise yourself and to contrast your self-image with the way you prefer to be. It also provides a chance to obtain an appraisal of yourself from another person you trust.

Step 1

Complete all the blanks in the "Self-appraisal." They are designed to help you describe your actual and preferred ways of reacting or relating to others and of leading. For each quality listed, check the scale on the left to find the number that best describes your actual behavior and write it in the first column. Then write the number that best describes the way you would prefer to act in the second column.

Step 2

Check the three items in each list on which you showed the greatest discrepancies between your actual and preferred ratings. If your preferred rating is higher than your actual rating, mark as a + (plus). If your actual rating is higher, mark - (minus). Circle the marks of those items you feel you presently can and want to improve in the most.

Step 3

Compare your self-perceptions with those of someone you trust who is willing to give you frank and genuine feedback.

| | Self-appraisal | | Feed- |
	Actual	Preferred	back

1. Style of Reacting

Tendency to Seek out Opportunities

Content to wait	1:2:3:4:5:6:7	Always searching	____	____	____

Breadth of Focus

Intensive, narrow focus on given problems	1:2:3:4:5:6:7	Extensive search for solutions on given problems	____	____	____

78

Speed of Decision
Defer judg-   Decide as
ment as long   quickly
as possible 1:2:3:4:5:6:7   as possible   _____   _____   _____

Intuitive vs Objective
Rely exclu-   Rely exclusively on   sively on
feelings   1:2:3:4:5:6:7   facts   _____   _____   _____

Impulsiveness
Think before   Speak before
I speak   1:2:3:4:5:6:7   I think   _____   _____   _____

Problem Solving
Always solve   Learn exclu-
problems for   sively from
myself   1:2:3:4:5:6:7   others   _____   _____   _____

Persistence
Give up too
quickly on
tough   Never give
problems   1:2:3:4:5:6:7   up   _____   _____   _____

Self-problem Identification
Never see   Always see
myself as   myself as
part of the   part of the
problem   1:2:3:4:5:6:7   problem   _____   _____   _____

External-Internal Focus
Completely   Completely
controlled   controlled
by my en-   by my inner
vironment   1:2:3:4:5:6:7   thoughts   _____   _____   _____

Understanding Why I Do What I Do
No under-   Complete
standing   1:2:3:4:5:6:7   understanding _____   _____   _____

79

Reactions, Success-Failure

Stimulated most by re- proof, failure, negative feedback 1:2:3:4:5:6:7	Stimulated most by praise, suc- cess, positive feedback	___	___	___

2. Style of Relating to Others

Ability to Listen to Others with Understanding

Inattentive/ unreceptive 1:2:3:4:5:6:7	Observant/ sensitive listener	___	___	___

Willingness to Share Feelings (Emotions) with Others

Completely unwilling 1:2:3:4:5:6:7	Completely willing	___	___	___

Awareness of the Feelings (Emotions) of Others

Completely Empathetic/ unaware 1:2:3:4:5:6:7	Sensitive responsive	___	___	___

Tolerance of Conflict and Antagonism

Not tolerant 1:2:3:4:5:6:7	Tolerant	___	___	___

Being Warm and Friendly to Others

Cold/ reserved 1:2:3:4:5:6:7	Warm/ outgoing	___	___	___

Acceptance of Affection and Warmth from Others

Uncom- fortable 1:2:3:4:5:6:7	Very com- fortable	___	___	___

| | Self-appraisal | | Feed- |
	Actual	Preferred	back

Reaction to Comments about My Behavior

Reject/ resentful/ defensive 1:2:3:4:5:6:7	Accept and grow	_____	_____	_____

Willingness to Trust Others

Very suspicious/ distrustful 1:2:3:4:5:6:7	Very trusting	_____	_____	_____

Ability to Influence Others

Completely unable 1:2:3:4:5:6:7	Completely able	_____	_____	_____

Relations with Peers

Very com- petitive 1:2:3:4:5:6:7	Very coop- erative	_____	_____	_____

3. Style of Leading

Risk Taking under Uncertainty

Extremely cautious 1:2:3:4:5:6:7	Extremely adventurous	_____	_____	_____

Delegation

Prefer to let others solve problems 1:2:3:4:5:6:7	Prefer to solve prob- lems myself	_____	_____	_____

Concern for Welfare of Subordinates

No concern at all 1:2:3:4:5:6:7	Complete concern	_____	_____	_____

Relations to Higher Authority

Always depend on higher authority 1:2:3:4:5:6:7	Always depend on myself, self-reliant	_____	_____	_____

		Self-appraisal		Feed-
		Actual	**Preferred**	**back**

Time Perspective

Short-run maximizer	1:2:3:4:5:6:7	Always con- sider the long-range view		
		___	___	___

Individual or Group Decisions

Prefer individual decisions	1:2:3:4:5:6:7	Prefer group decisions		
		___	___	___

Political Vs. Participative

Rely on political alli- ances, deals, bluffs	1:2:3:4:5:6:7	Rely on6 open com- munication, involvement, trust		
		___	___	___

**Use of Authority in Getting
Work Done**

Rely on my position and power	1:2:3:4:5:6:7	Rely on persuasion personal skill and knowledge		
		___	___	___

Task vs. Human Relations Concerns

Exclusively concerned with getting job done	1:2:3:4:5:6:7	Primarily concerned with main- taining good relations	___	___	___

Exercise 5.3: Personal Effectiveness for Leadership

Active and effective individuals display a set of fairly common characteristics. In the same way, others continually display a set of characteristics regularly associated with being less active or effective. This exercise is designed to help you see where you stand.

On the left side of the scale are the characteristics of inactive and ineffective people and on the right side the characteristics of the active and effective. On the scale circle the number where you think you are.

You can do this exercise individually and then get honest feedback from a colleague you trust. If the exercise is done in a small group of your choice, share your ratings of one another, giving reasons or explanations for the ratings with concrete examples from your style of being or behaving.

Inactive/Ineffective		Active/Effective
1. I am usually passive and lack energy and vitality.	1:2:3:4:5:6:7	I am usually active and have a high energy level.
2. I avoid "stretching" experiences.	1:2:3:4:5:6:7	I continually try to stretch myself.
3. I avoid challenge and seek to be undisturbed.	1:2:3:4:5:6:7	I seek challenge.
4. I am largely influenced by the views of others.	1:2:3:4:5:6:7	I am clear about my personal values and priorities.
5. I set low personal standards.	1:2:3:4:5:6:7	I set high personal standards.

6. I misuse time and energy.	1:2:3:4:5:6:7	I use time and energy as valuable resources.
7. I avoid self-knowledge and insight.	1:2:3:4:5:6:7	I continually seek self-knowledge and insight into myself.
8. I avoid feedback.	1:2:3:4:5:6:7	I welcome feedback.
9. I opt out when the going gets tough.	1:2:3:4:5:6:7	I always see things through.
10. I am generally dis-satisfied with others.	1:2:3:4:5:6:7	I generally get along well with others.
11. I never show concern for others.	1:2:3:4:5:6:7	I continually show concern for others.
12. I am always tense.	1:2:3:4:5:6:7	I am always relaxed and calm.
13. I tend to manipulate others.	1:2:3:4:5:6:7	I am always open and honest.
14. I am basically unhappy with my life.	1:2:3:4:5:6:7	I am basically happy with my life.

The above two sets of characteristics (left and right) become stark alternatives when placed side by side. They are, in reality, choices that we have to make about ourselves, our approach to life and our approach to work. Few people exhibit either an extremely active or an extremely passive approach to life. Most individuals fall somewhere in the middle of the scale. Personal growth and development are the results of moving away from the passive towards the active. Active and effective people tend to find life an adventure, enjoy variety and always seem to end up enriched. On the other hand, passive and ineffective people seem always to be in a state of inadequate adjustment to the unsatisfactory nature of things. And active people make better and dynamic leaders.

Note for Teachers

During this century there has been an explosion of knowledge, and educational systems all over the world concentrated on imparting this capability with great skill. Consequently, in discussion of the relative importance of knowledge and character, many individuals raise questions about knowledge having a value of merely about 10 percent of a leader's total capability. They feel that the percentage should be higher. To allocate such a precise percentage can, of course, be questioned, but the truth is that difficult decisions can be taken only by strength of character, and that is why character plays such a dominant role in the capability of a leader. The real test of a leader comes when a chosen course of action has to be implemented in the face of difficulties, discouragements, criticism, adversity and human failures. In such situations, it is character that helps a leader to stay the course.

The exercises about self-knowledge are useful as indicators. At the end of these exercises, it is necessary for a teacher to spend time individually with each student to pinpoint his or her major strengths and weaknesses. This is the most difficult role for the teacher and requires a great deal of patience, privacy and love. Self-knowledge is the stepping-stone for self-improvement and consequently has to be handled in a way that an action program, such as the one discussed in the case study in chapter 7, can be developed.

6

To Be: Universal Inner Structure of Good Leaders: Dealing with People

Dealing appropriately with people is the crux of the entire leadership process. Its effectiveness depends on the strength and balance of the universal inner structure of the leader. Fully realizing this fact is essential. Diagrammatically, the relationship between inner structure and leadership is depicted in figure 6.1.

The goal of a leader should be to strengthen his or her inner structure to such an extent that the leader can get the best out of people in "victory as well as in defeat." Before we discuss how to strengthen this structure, it is appropriate to examine some facets of ability to deal with people. We shall discuss the following in this chapter:

- Dealing with people at various levels

- Human nature

- *Mahamantra* (the ultimate formula) for dealing with people

- Importance of communication

- Leadership style

- Leadership in a global context

- Practical hints for dealing with people

Dealing with People at Various Levels

The Stanford Research Institute has quantified the importance of understanding people and dealing with them appropriately as management technology for 88 percent of effective management (leadership) strategy. It is well to remember that this truth is applicable at all levels of leadership—junior, middle and senior. The "Katz Model"[1] in figure 6.2 shows the relevant value of management skills at various levels. Although there have been some minor changes in the original design, it clearly shows that human relations skill is consistency the biggest component at all levels of management.

A leader in any organization has to handle people in the following three different directions:

1. *Downwards*—building his or her own team into an effective and cohesive group motivated to achieve the goals of the organization

2. *Laterally*—winning the support and cooperation of colleagues over whom the leader has no control but who have an important functional relationship with the group or organization headed by him or her

3. *Upwards*—maintaining a purposeful, constructive and harmonious relationship with the higher authority under whom a leader functions—the boss

Human Nature

In order to deal with people effectively, it is useful for a leader to understand human nature. There are a large number of theories about it. For developing leadership potential, it is useful to focus our attention on two concepts that have lasting and practical value for leaders.

ABILITY TO DEAL WITH PEOPLE
THE ROLE OF UNIVERSAL
INNER STRUCTURE OF GOOD LEADERS

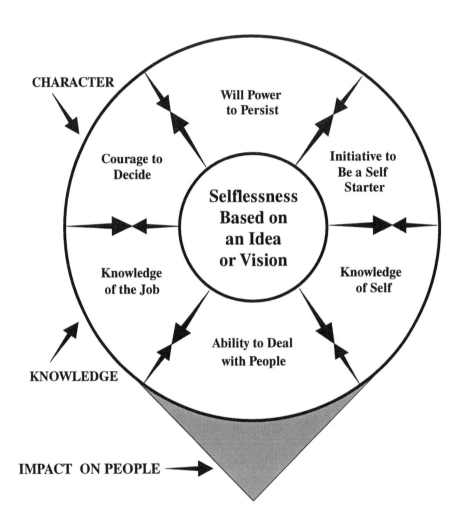

Figure 6.1

SKILLS OF EFFECTIVE EXECUTIVES

KATZ MODEL

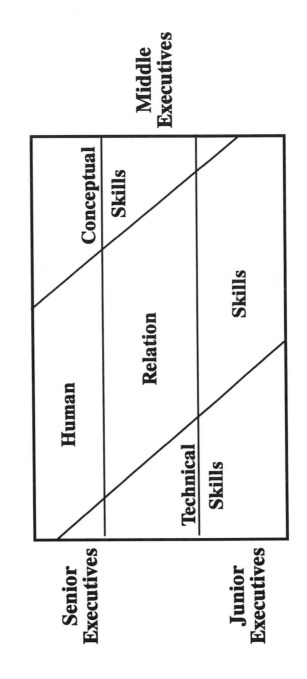

Figure 6.2

Recent research suggests that "you and I motivate ourselves to a large extent by responding to inner needs." In this context, Maslow's concept of hierarchy of needs is useful. He suggests that individual needs are arranged as in figure 6.3—the strongest ones at the bottom and the weaker, but more motivating, ones at the top. In his later years Maslow also focused on spiritual needs that have been the basis of the Indian culture, ethos and civilization for 6,000 years; these needs motivate a person to acts of great dedication, self-sacrifice and service to lofty ideals and causes.

The second concept is the Indian experience that the nature of every individual is a mixture of the following three *gunas* (characteristics):

- *Tamas*—the dull, lazy and inert quality

- *Rajas*—the active, passionate aspect of nature

- *Satwic*—the pure, ethical aspect of nature, aiming at harmony and balance

Desire for benefits and fruits of action is a sign of *rajas*; the giving up of action because you cannot get any benefits is *tamas*. To engage oneself in action, knowing that results will follow, and yet not be attached to them or get concerned by them is *satwa*. Indian civilization and culture have survived because of the high value attached to *satwic* leadership in our society. *Satwic* leaders have always exercised great influence on Indian minds and actions—the latest example of a such a leader being Mahatma Gandhi.

'Mahamantra' for Dealing with People

There is a simple sentence to guide leaders in dealing with people. But, in its significance, it is so potent that it has acquired the status of a *mahamantra* (a great formula). It is:

MASLOW'S NEED HIERARCHY

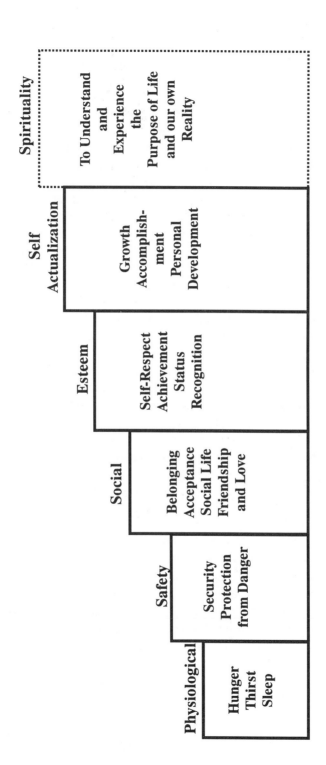

Figure 6.3

A good leader knows his or her people better than
their mothers do and cares even more

No one knows the nature of a group of people better than a
mother knows her children. She has a full intuitive feel for their
needs. She knows their weaknesses and their strengths. Her main
concern, and very often the only concern, is to bring them up in a
manner that makes them an asset to the family, the community, the
country and the world. The clearer and higher the vision of a
mother, the loftier is her effort to groom her children to excellence.
With the intimate knowledge of their total personality, she knows
who will do the right thing merely by watching her example; who
will need a pat on the back, or perhaps a quiet chat, and which
one, now and then, may well need the rod. She uses the rod with
love, to correct mistakes and bad habits. The most pronounced
factor that makes the children amenable to the guiding hand of the
mother is the fact that she cares and that they implicitly trust her.

The same has to be the approach of an effective leader towards
his or her people. If they are convinced that the leader is a person
who knows them well and truly cares for them, they will do
anything for him or her. However, it requires a very major effort
to know people and know them better than even their own
mothers—effort in terms of time, attention and genuine interest in
people. (A self-assessment exercise about knowing people is at the
end of this chapter. The purpose of the exercise is to bring home
to you the need for devoting time and effort to knowing people).

The difference between *indulgence* and *caring* should be clearly
understood. *Indulgence* means "excessive gratification, giving
material things"—money, conveniences and so on. Indulgence, by
and large, spoils the recipients. Caring, on the other hand, is a
matter of attitude; it is a quality based on unselfish love.
Consequently, caring is a matter of the heart and is not related to

material resources. A skill that often helps a leader to know and care for his or her people is the skill of communication.

Communication: Knowing People

The ability to know people is the starting point in dealing with them, and communication skill plays an important role in this ability. There are detailed courses on communication in the syllabi of educational programs. These courses help a leader *to tell* what he or she wants done. However, some essential features of this skill relevant to knowing and handling people need discussion.

Most strained and fractured relations can be traced to mutual breakdown of communication between individuals in a family, group, community or country and even among the community of nations. One starts seeing only the uglier side of others, and it leads to alienation. The ability to communicate, on the other hand, puts human relations on an even keel by removing misperceptions and misunderstandings. The ability has two sides:

- Skill of expression

- Skill of listening

The skill of expression does not merely mean the gift of gab or cleverness with words. For a leader, expression is a vehicle used to generate trust. Verbal expression counts for only 30 percent of this skill; the balance, 70 percent, is body language—expression in the eyes, conviction in the tone, sincerity in the posture, and generally, vibrations a person conveys. Body language communicates the total being of a leader, and its effectiveness depends entirely on the strength and balance of the universal inner structure of good leaders. In genuine expression there can be no pretension. Spontaneity, straightforwardness and sincerity are far more effective than sheer command over the language.

The skill of listening means understanding and knowing the other person. It has been found that this part of communication is even more important, but, unfortunately, less prevalent. "Watch your listen/talk ratio—learn to be a good listener"[2] is sound advice. Listen with your ears and observe body language with your eyes. Even nature has a design in the listen-talk ratio. It gives two ears to a person, but only one mouth!

Listening has three ingredients. The first, of course, is the physical process of hearing what the other person is saying; this involves attention. Comprehending what the person is saying is the second ingredient, and demands undivided attention. Looking out of the window or attending to routine papers while listening are signs of inattentiveness. Remembering what you hear is the third ingredient of this skill and, naturally, comes about only if a leader hears and comprehends what is said. The ability to listen attentively and sympathetically with signs of warmth makes the other person feel that he is an individual and not merely an *it*, a faceless part of the machine. This helps generate trust in the team. Above all, "listening to the body language with eyes" gives a leader an opportunity to really know his or her people and their characteristics.

Remembering names is an important part of communication. There is no sweeter music to the ears of a person than his or her own name especially when being addressed by the boss.

Experience shows that effective communication means:

50 percent listening
25 percent speaking
15 percent reading
10 percent writing

Leadership Styles

Sound is the statement that a good leader varies his or her style from authoritarian to participative (autocratic to democratic, if you like), depending on the task, the changing situation encountered, and the composition of the group led. It sums up, rather pithily, the way a good leader has to function. However, no effective leader ever consciously adopts a style. It comes, and indeed must come, naturally from within. It is the expression of the person and the strength and balance of his or her universal inner structure. Anyone who tries to project what he or she is not is bound to suffer a setback. It is better "to be yourself" than to try to copy a style.

Conceptually, the changes in style that spread between the two extremes is well depicted in the model evolved by R. Tannenbaum and W. Smidt, shown in figure 6.4. It should be looked at only as an illustration depicting the range of options available. In practice, any change in style is merely an intuitive variation in the mix of personal example, persuasion and compulsion.

Personal example is the most potent factor in inspiring people to do what they are expected to do. If a leader can work 12 to 14 hours a day, then the message will get across. Personal example in punctuality, integrity, honesty, frugality, courage, persistence, initiative, unselfish love of people or whatever is infectious. *To do* yourself what you preach is the secret of leading people.

There are people who need persuasion and times when persuasion is necessary to motivate people to do what has to be done. When they understand the circumstances, people do rise to the occasion and go through the most irksome tasks. Long-term persuasion lies in an organizational culture (esprit de corps) in which people take pride in doing anything to uphold the honor and good name of the organization.

LEADERSHIP STYLES

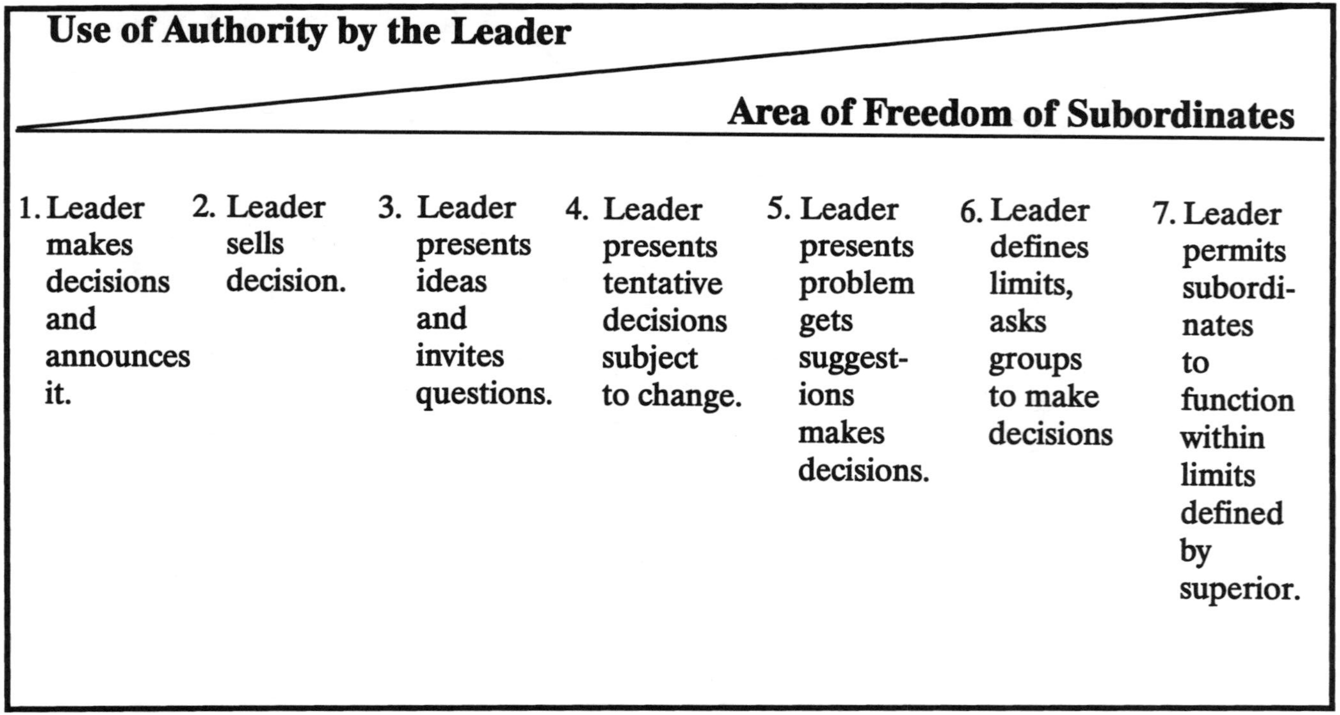

Use of Authority by the Leader				Area of Freedom of Subordinates		
1. Leader makes decisions and announces it.	2. Leader sells decision.	3. Leader presents ideas and invites questions.	4. Leader presents tentative decisions subject to change.	5. Leader presents problem gets suggest-ions makes decisions.	6. Leader defines limits, asks groups to make decisions	7. Leader permits subordi-nates to function within limits defined by superior.

Figure 6.4

Compulsion by punishing the few indolent, lazy or resentful individuals who do not perform their share of work is also necessary to maintain discipline, as is letting people know unambiguously that the leader is fair and just, but not tolerant of the incompetent, the crooked and the mischievous. Inability to take appropriate action is often rationalized by pointing to pressure from the top, fear of litigation, trade union agitation and so on. To a degree, such failure is also due to lack of moral courage to act.

Leadership in Global Context

In the decades ahead, mankind will start making rapid progress towards its ultimate goal: Unity of Man, Global Economy and Earth Citizenship.

The widespread ethnic and religious conflicts that we see in the world today are the last-ditch resistance to the new world order. Even major upheavals predicted for the twenty-first century— "demographic explosion, turbulence of economic leveling and ecological catastrophes"[3] will only accelerate the march of humanity.

In the universe, the planet Earth is "like a big building divided into rooms with walls. One room is labeled America, another India and yet another China and so on. You remove the walls and we are all in one big hall. With love and adjustment we can all learn to live happily together."[4] The basic goal of all cultures is the same—"to be human."[5] It is important, therefore, that the leaders of tomorrow prepare themselves to be in harmony with this great transition.

More than 2,000 years ago, India was going through a similar experience on a smaller scale. It had become a melting pot for different faiths and ethnic groups who, over the centuries, had migrated to this land of plenty and prosperity. Conflict is built into any such process. But its remedy is also available—the remedy lies in the hearts of people.

The leaders of tomorrow would do well to understand the spiritual heritage of humanity. If we read books like *The Perennial Philosophy* by Aldous Huxley or *Sathya Sai Baba: The Embodiment of Love* by Peggy Mason and Ron Laing, we can understand the basis for the unity of man—nay, the unity of universe. Such books enlarge our vision to the far horizons that we are capable of perceiving. Leaders would then be able to rise above their national, ethnic or religious origin. By conviction and action, they would be able to project themselves as world citizens—like, for example, Jimmy Carter, ex-president of the USA; Willy Brandt, former chancellor of Germany; or Mahatma Gandhi of India.

In the ancient world Emperor Ashoka ruled over most of India. Like the USA today, the country then was a melting pot of cultures. Ashoka had the following edict etched on rocks in all parts of India.

> All sects deserve reverence for one reason or another. By thus acting, man exalts his or her own sect, and at the same time does service to the sects of other people.[6]

Only leaders with a vision of unity in diversity will be able to command respect of people in the "global village" of tomorrow. Those who want to experience such a vision and attitude being translated into daily life should visit a place in India called Prasanthi Nilayam, the abode of Sri Sathya Sai Baba. Thousands of people from all over the world are thronging there to experience this unity.

PRACTICAL HINTS ON DEALING WITH PEOPLE

The operative part of leadership capability lies in the ability to deal with people in a manner that encourages them to give their best for a cause, an organization or the task at hand. This capability depends on the strength and balance of *to be* in a leader—his universal inner structure of effective leadership. Reinforcing this structure is within the reach of anyone who applies himself or herself to this exciting endeavor with *sincerity* and *willpower* till transformation takes place. Even while making an effort to improve the source of leadership, those who want to be more effective will find a few practical hints on dealing with people valuable.

Most of the hints discussed in this section are based on practical experience of leaders in various walks of life. The hints are designed to help leaders to deal with people working for them, their colleagues and their boss. A good leader never looks at these people as his or her subordinates; they are considered as members of his or her team. The dominant virtue in dealing with people is unselfish love like that of a good and affectionate mother; even when she uses the rod, her motive is corrective and not punitive.

Dealing with People Working for a Leader

Self-control. No team captain can hope to control and inspire a team unless he or she learns to self-control and self-discipline. This is a difficult task, but without it, there is little chance for a person to become a successful leader. Self-control requires a certain amount of philosophic outlook and frugality, which is often associated with aristocrats and saints, and not only adds to leadership potential but also is a source of great happiness.

Success and failure. It is a basic trait of human nature that an individual attributes successes of an organization to the parts he or she played and blames failures on the system. On the other hand, a good leader gives credit to his or her people for successes and takes responsibility for failures. This approach binds people together in a collective effort to work for the organization.

Setting targets. It is useful to let the individuals themselves set targets for their work. In this event, not only are they likely to meet these targets but even surpass them.

Correcting mistakes. A leader often has to correct people who falter, show traces of weakness, or fail. It is better to say, "This is not what I expected from a person of your caliber and ability" than to say, "What else could I expect from a blockhead like you." The first approach enhances a person's self-respect, even in failure. The second makes him or her your enemy.

We and not you. A good leader always projects himself or herself as a part of a team and invariably talks in terms of "we" and not "you."

Accessibility. It is a leader's responsibility to ensure that he or she is accessible. The leader should institutionalize the time and place for meeting the members of his or her team. Tragedies and illnesses are a frequent occurrence in human life. A good leader makes it a point to find time for seeing people who are afflicted or who have difficult problems to tackle. Visiting them when they are hospitalized should also be a matter of priority time allocation. You win lasting commitment from people thus handled.

Anger. A good leader does not lose his or her temper. However, righteous anger is very different from uncontrolled rage and should not be suppressed. But special care should be taken to uphold the honor and dignity of an individual in the presence of colleagues and family members.

Recognition. Good and effective leaders have used the human urge for recognition with telling effect to foster interpersonal bonds with people and to motivate them. Leaders have scrupulously used the principle 'Praise in Public and Reprimand in Private' to create an organizational culture in which people work much beyond the call of duty to maintain excellence in their organization. The real basis for making individuals feel like heroes is, of course, genuine care and unselfish love by the leader for his or her people. Some of the practices that have been used with good effect in this field are:

- Smile and greet people by their names. There is no sweeter music to a person's ears than hearing his or her own name. *Kaya hall hai, Sham Singh?* (How are you, Sham Singh?) will get a warm response and commitment if you can add, *Tumhare bete Sunder Singh ki parhai kese chal rahi hai?* (How is your son Sunder Singh doing in his studies?). Then Sham Singh's day is made and his dedication assured. If these brief interactions are in the native language of the person spoken to, then the effect will be even more lasting.

- Be on the lookout to spot good work that can be praised. When you notice it, then promptly give credit to the person in front of his or her colleagues. In special cases, have him or her photographed with yourself, or even with the chief executive. However, never let sloppy work go unchecked. And always be sure to tell off the guilty party in private.

- Show personal interest in the development of your people and their careers. Guide and help them to improve their skills.

- Select an employee of the month and display his or her photograph on the bulletin board. This practice has a very positive impact but should be done only for persons who genuinely do good work.

- Occasionally join your people and eat lunch along with them.

- Call your people in small groups for tea or a meal at your home.

- Introduce your people to seniors or visitors, pointing out and praising their strong points and achievements.

- On completion of a project or a special task, write a note of thanks to every member of the group for his or her contribution.

- Get photographs of your people in the company magazine, if there is one, or in the media.

- Create symbols of teamwork—like a T-shirt with a logo or lapel in the shape of a company logo—to inculcate a spirit of dedication. A number of public and private sector companies have the same uniform for their entire staff from the CEO right down to shop floor workers.

- Give recognition promptly. To be effective, recognition needs to be timely. The military has a system of immediate battlefield bravery awards. Right after a battle, these awards are given by senior commanders to the few individuals who have performed beyond the call of duty. This invariably leads to high morale.

Dealing with Colleagues

These are difficult people to handle. Competition, jealousy and one-upmanship take their toll. However, there are a few practices that pay handsome dividends:

Be a team player. Always help your colleagues in their tasks and projects. A good team player always gets positive response. Do unto them what you expect them to do unto you is the soundest practice.

Don't take unfair advantage. Anyone who seeks an unfair advantage over his or her colleagues is labeled a climber or *safarshi* (person using pull) and earns hostility. A good leader avoids this.

Dealing with the Boss

An effective leader develops the skill needed to maintain a good relationship with his or her boss. Some practical tips for this are:

- Know your boss's background, career, habits, methodology of work, aspirations, likes and dislikes. It enables you to anticipate his or her moods and wishes, and that invariably is appreciated.

- Be dependable. When you undertake an assignment, you must do everything humanly possible to complete it successfully. No boss really cares for a subordinate whose performance is uncertain. Honest mistakes can be tolerated, but unreliability cannot be entertained. If you run into insurmountable difficulties in completing an assignment, then it is best that you inform the boss yourself, rather than letting the boss learn about it from other sources.

- Listen to your boss with undivided attention. Establish eye contact with the boss to focus your undivided attention on what he or she is saying. Stop formulating in your mind responses that you feel will meet with his or her approval; this distracts attention from attentive listening. Read your boss's body language to comprehend not only what is being said but also what is implied. Before you respond, pause in order to fully digest and understand what has been conveyed. No boss likes a subordinate who has to be told things twice.

- Speak briefly, emphasizing the essentials to convey your thoughts clearly, so that you get full value out of the time you have to interact with your boss. It requires forethought. A good aid is to reduce the most complex problems to a one-page memo.

- Be diplomatic. Offer options for handling a problem, with the pros and cons well articulated. It is more than likely that the boss will select the option you prefer. Never reject out of hand what he or she suggests. Raise observations in the form of questions: Will it not cause disruption of the schedule? Do we have people to implement such a sophisticated approach? and so on.

- Gently point out the inherent dangers. To be diplomatic does not mean letting the boss make bad moves. It is much better to be sincere. In the long run, such sincerity wins the respect of the boss more than mere flattery.

- Let your boss look good. It is wise to highlight his or her strengths to others. Before a meeting or a conference, give the boss all the information or input well in advance and let him or her do the talking. During a meeting don't offer any fresh information unless your boss invites you to speak. Don't be afraid to let the boss take credit for your ideas. In the long run, it will be good for your relationship with him or her.

- Be a team player. While speaking about colleagues, highlight their good points rather than their weaknesses. You will gain in genuine respect.

- Solve your problems. A subordinate who is a problem solver is preferred to the one who is weepy.

In the ultimate analysis, handling people is a matter of attitude. It is expecting the utmost from them while caring for them completely. Such an attitude is possible only if a leader can create an atmosphere in which there is free communication. Tolerating shirkers and parasites in the name of "being human" does a great deal of damage. They must be dealt with strictly. Fortunately, however, such people are few and far between.

There is no better commentary on leadership and a leader's relationship with the people he or she leads than what Sun Tzu wrote more than 2,000 years ago:

And, therefore, the general who in advancing does not seek personal fame, and in withdrawing is not concerned with avoiding punishment, but whose only purpose is to protect the people and promote the best interests of his sovereign is the precious jewel of the state.

Because such a general regards his men as infants, they will march with him into the deepest valleys. He treats them as his beloved sons and they will die with him.

If he cherishes his men in this way, he will gain their utmost strength.

Exercise 6.1: A Leader Knows His or Her People Better Than Their Mothers

Fill in the following questionnaire for any individual in your class. If you know an answer, then write it as in item 1. below. Otherwise, put an x.

Name of selected person_____

1. Name of paternal grandfather__*Tom Sanders*_____

2. Name of paternal grandmother_____

3. Name of maternal grandfather_____

4. Name of maternal grandmother_____

5. Religion_____

6. Hometown/village_____

7. School where studied first four years_____

8. Father's name_____

9. Father's profession/work_____

10. Mother's name_____

11. Mother's profession/work_____

12. Education of father_____

13. Education of mother_____

14. Names of brothers/sisters

    (a) _____

    (b) _____

    (c) _____

    (d) _____

15. Classes in which they are studying or their qualifications

    (a) _____

    (b) _____

    (c) _____

    (d) _____

16. What does your classmate want to become in life?

_____

17. What is his or her strongest virtue?_____

18. What is his or her worst weakness? _____

19. Have you visited his or her home? _____

20. What is his or her best game? _____

21. What are his or her hobbies? _____

Scoring

1. Item 1 is an example and does not count towards the score. Give one mark for knowing the detail asked for in each item. If your score is 16 or more, you have potential for developing the ability to deal with people. Otherwise, you need to devote more time to this.

2. The purpose of this exercise is to give you a feel for how well a leader has to know his or people.

_____

Note for Teachers

If possible, students should be shown the Warner Brothers film entitled *Twelve O'Clock High,* which is available on video. This classic film with Gregory Peck as the hero is based on the performance of a bomber group in the U.S. Air Force during World War II. The film shows the performance of two leaders in dealing with people. Both are very high-quality officers. And yet the first one leads the group to low morale, high casualties and virtual unfitness for war. At that point the first leader is replaced by the second one, who turns the situation around.

Before starting the film ask students to note the reasons for the poor performance of the group. Also, ask them to prepare themselves to give the steps they would take to restore the group to peak efficiency if selected to replace the first leader.

It is useful to break the film into three parts. First, stop the film, just after the first leader is replaced and hold a discussion on the observations students were asked to make. Stop the film again when the group regains its fighting effectiveness. After this second part, there should be a discussion on the steps the replacement takes.

The third part is battle scenes from actual combat and may be shown if time is available.

Encourage students to add practical hints for dealing with people after discussing the topic with their parents.

7
Strengthening *To Be* for Good Leadership

Take care of your thoughts. Then, actions will take care of themselves. You sow an action and reap a tendency. You sow a tendency and reap a habit. You sow your habit and reap your character. You sow your character and reap your destiny. Therefore, destiny is in your own hands.[1]

We now come to the most important content of this book: How to improve our leadership potential?

In the earlier chapters we discussed what, in holistic and practical terms, leadership is—what the process of leadership is, what its functions are, and what components of leadership are universal.

We learned that knowledge was an essential component of good leadership. It is not very difficult to acquire and update our knowledge. The educational and training systems of the world are geared to impart knowledge in all fields of work. It is important that knowledge and skills related to our work are constantly updated. For example, taking advantage of courses by correspondence, short training programs, seminars or workshops, as well as reading professional books and magazines, which are available in abundance. A potential leader should make full use of these facilities. However, we also discussed that, although knowledge was important, it counted for only 12 percent of the whole potential of a leader. Character is by far the biggest component of leadership. It is precisely here that the real difficulty in improving leadership arises. Unfortunately, there is no way by which anyone can be transformed in the classroom into a person of character. The description of a man of character bears repetition. He is:

An honest man;

a man with a sense of duties and obligations of his position, whatever it may be;

a man who tells the truth;

a man who gives others their due;

a man considerate to the weak;

a man who has principles and stands by them;

a man not too elated by good fortune, and not too depressed by bad;

a man who is loyal;

a man who can be trusted.[2]

Are Leaders Born or Made?

The question that arises is: How can we transform ourselves to become worthy of being called a person of character? Can it be done at all? It is this dilemma that gives rise to a perpetual debate on whether leaders are born or made. The best answer to this question may well be found by discussing a similar problem: Are Olympic athletes born or made? The answer is that no one can be an Olympian without having some basic athletic aptitude and then developing that aptitude through intense and dedicated training. And only through training, commitment and tenacity can the level of excellence a person can attain be determined. The same is the case with leadership. Through training young people with aptitude, a large number of good athletes and sportsmen can be produced, even though Olympians may be few and far between and Gold Medal winners still fewer. Similarly, training can help most of us become good and effective leaders even though outstanding ones may be rare. In both cases the level of excellence depends on the effort an individual makes at developing himself or herself.

Strengthening Leadership Potential

Since leadership is exercised by the mind (reflected in character), it is the mind that has to be trained to develop qualities that add up to the total leadership potential. Since Western research on leadership became fragmented, there is not much help that we can get from that source. However, one well-known psychologist reiterates a time-tested technique for drawing inspiration to improve and develop ourself—reading about the lives of outstanding leaders. He says:

> The would-be leader should study what is known about leadership and read books on leadership. He should examine himself in respect of attributes of leadership which he learns about, try to adjust himself, first in behavior and presently, to the ideal attitude. There is no doubt that wisdom backed up by a desire to learn, can effect great changes in ability to lead other men.[3]

So the first technique for developing our leadership potential is to read widely about leadership, with a special emphasis on the lives of outstanding leaders in history. The Management Development Institute in India is carrying out studies on the outstanding enterprise leaders of contemporary India. One of the studies undertaken was on Rusi Modi, the former chairman of Tata Iron and Steel Company (TISCO), which is one of the best run enterprises in the country. Rusi has been repeatedly rated as an outstanding chief executive in India and is well recognized as one of the best in the world. A firm believer in the idea that leaders are born, not made, Modi expressed his views while appearing on a television show. When he reiterated his belief on this issue, the interviewer asked his advice on steps an executive could take to

111

develop his or her potential to the maximum. He paused and reflected for a while. And then he suddenly recalled his school days. As a boy he was very fond of reading about the lives of leaders like Bismarck and Napoleon. It naturally influenced his behavior, even as a boy. He recounted how, at times, his father would chastise him for behaving like a Napoleon! The lives of these great men had certainly inspired him. Rusi's experience is very similar to that of a large number of leaders who have subconsciously been influenced by the lives of great men.

Anyone whose ambition is to transform himself or herself, to do well should read about the lives of outstanding people—particularly in the field of his or her own work specialization. A list of 108 great lives in the history of humanity is at the end of this book. Many more could be added to it. To buy the biographies or autobiographies of our favorite leaders is one of the best investments we can make. But it is of value only if we acquire the reading habit. And this was the problem faced by the author—a general in the Indian Army, who undertook research on how to improve leadership. He knew that a good proportion of his officers were shy of reading!

The search for a structured way of transforming people led him to find a gold mine in India's spiritual heritage and its experience with reprogramming the human character. The concept of *sadhana* (meaning "persistent effort to achieve particular results") has been used for thousands of years to improve human beings. It is achieved by purging weaknesses and vices and integrating correct human values into a person's character. The following safe advice articulating this ancient technique of remaking a person opened a window in the author's search:

> You have a particular way of writing vertically. This is *prarabhda* (an inherited situation, condition or tendency). You can change that writing to a slanting way. This is *purushartha* (effort). Take care of your

112

thoughts. Then your actions will take care of themselves. Action follows thought. *You sow an action and reap a tendency. You sow a tendency and reap a habit. You sow a habit and reap a character. You sow your character and reap your destiny. Therefore, destiny is your own creation. If you change your habits, you can become master of your destiny.*[4]

The essence of this ancient message is that we can improve our character if we are prepared to undertake a deliberate program to change our habits. Interestingly, the doyen of management teachers, Peter Drucker, has arrived at exactly the same conclusion. He says that "self-development of effective executives is central to development of the organization, whether it be a business, a government agency, a research laboratory, a hospital or a military service. As executives work towards becoming effective, they raise the performance level of the whole organization. They raise the sights of people, their own as well as others."[5] This process means "he has to learn a good many new work habits as he proceeds along his career, and he will occasionally have to unlearn some old work habits."[6] Self-development really means developing "leadership—not the leadership of brilliance and genius, to be sure, but the much more modest yet enduring leadership of dedication, determination and serious purpose."[7]

Unfortunately, leadership, particularly its major component, *to be*, which is the source of effectiveness, cannot be taught. It is an art that can be acquired only by self-effort. Leadership is a function of interpersonal relations and not of organizational status. The question that arises is how an individual who wishes to develop his leadership ability should go about training himself?

Drucker categorically asserts that effectiveness can be learned and suggests: "Effectiveness, in other words, is a habit that is a complex of practices. And practices can always be learned.

Practices one learns by practicing and practicing and practicing again."[8]

In his seminal work *The Seven Habits of Highly Effective People,* the author, Stephen Covey, concentrates on habit changing by those who wish to become effective leaders.[9] The theme of the book is an extract from the paragraph quoted above (the portion in italics). It is quite obvious that the Indian experience of transforming human personality is being adopted worldwide. India's contribution in this field is well in keeping with the ancient Indian prayer *Lokaa Samasthaa Sukhino Bhavantu* (May all the world enjoy peace and comfort). It is this ideal that has helped Indian civilization survive for 6,000 years.

It is comparatively easy to practice music, drama, sports, athletics and so on, as the improvements can be displayed and progress monitored. But how can we practice the intangibles, the virtues of character? It is precisely in this instance that the concept of *sadhana*, designed essentially to transform human mind and character, is a help. Spiritual aspirants are encouraged to maintain a diary. The experience of this technique is that anyone who follows the discipline of maintaining a diary with honesty and determination meets with "unfailing success." The technique involves a deliberate decision to identify weaknesses we wish to eradicate from our behavior and virtues or habits we wish to inculcate. Having done so, we have to prepare a simple diary to record the effort we make everyday to achieve our goals. Every evening we have to spend a few minutes reflecting on our attempts to reach the goals during the course of the day. And then we have to record that effort appropriately. The starting point for a diary is self-knowledge, as discussed in chapter 5. Once we know the weaknesses we wish to eradicate and virtues to be imbibed, then making a diary is a relatively simple matter. A case study will illustrate this technique. However, before reading the case study, it would be useful to see two sample diaries. One is found in this chapter, and a second that was designed by Benjamin Franklin, the well-known founding father of the USA, is included in the brief sketch of his life in chapter 8.

Self-Development Diary

The layout of the self-development diary, created in 1979, is presented in table 7.1. It is only a model that can be modified to suit individual needs. The areas of the universal inner structure of good leaders that need reinforcement will differ from one person to another. So also, the weaknesses that have to be eradicated will be different. Consequently, for each person the checklist in the diary will have to be structured according to his or her needs.

Out of the experience of the last 14 years, one modification has emerged. Most individuals like to focus their attention on absorbing one virtue and/or eradicating one weakness at a time. This practice is essentially based on the experience of Benjamin Franklin, who had used the diary as an aid in transforming himself. The secret of success lies in setting simple and limited goals in the first instance and achieving success in these. By doing so, "we build the strength of character, the being that makes possible every other positive thing in our lives."[10] This is well illustrated in the case of Vishnu Prasad of Nepal. (See after Table 7.1).

Table 7.1: A Model of Leadership—Self-development Diary

	Month_____	
No.	1 2 3 4...31	Remarks
1. Time devoted to physical fitness		
2. Time devoted to study for acquiring professional skills		
3. Time devoted to studying people under me and people management		

4. Number of subordinates I have helped in their personal and professional development

5. Number of times when I had the choice and placed the good of the organization/country above my self-interest

6. Number of times I had the courage to correct my subordinates' mistakes/discipline them

7. Number of occasions I set a personal example for my subordinates

8. Time wasted in fantasies of family, fortune and fame in the future, or in fretting about the past

9. Number of times I have been greedy, angry, jealous, envious or hateful

10. Number of acts of self-denial used to build up my willpower

---

Self-Development Diary: A Case Study

Vishnu Prasad was a trainee executive in an international bank in Kathmandu. He had done so well that he was selected for this job even before he was 21 years old—he had been a good student. The bank organized a three-day leadership workshop based on the model in this book. Prasad was one of the 20 participants.

At the end of the workshop, the participants were asked to set themselves the goal of changing one or two habits in the next three months. Each participant was given individual help to crystallize their goals. Prasad was honest enough to explain his problems to the teacher in these words:

> I am from a very poor family living in Eastern Nepal. My brother in the Indian Army supported me when I came for college studies to Kathmandu. I was a good student; many well-to-do boys of the town tried to befriend me. I used to be ashamed of my poor background. So I started painting a false picture about my parents. Slowly, it became a habit to tell lies and half-truths when it came to projecting my self-image. This habit has extended to telling lies about my achievements to impress others. The result is that I have all the time concocted stories. This habit has led me to another problem. To increase my popularity, I readily offer to do things for others, but then I realize that I have neither the time nor the resources to do what I promised. And to get out of such a situation, I spin more yarns. All this bothers me. I know deep inside me that it is wrong, but I just cannot give it up.

After some discussion with a teacher in the workshop, he decided upon a goal to be achieved in three months: "I would not tell a lie." He made a simple diary for this one-point program. Every evening he would take stock of the day and count the number of incorrect statements that he made during the day. He would record the score in his diary. And then resolve to reduce the score the next day.

During the first fortnight, the average came to four incorrect statements per day. It fell to three during the second fortnight, and stayed at three during the third. But it fell to one during the fourth. During the fifth fortnight, he recorded only two such occasions in all 15 days; and these two occurred when he was under great stress, fearful that the truth might damage his standing with his manager. He persisted, and in the last fortnight had a

117

clean diary for all 15 days. He learned to keep quiet when his past habit prompted him to spin a yarn. For the next three months, he added one more item to his diary—to own up whenever he made a mistake. Initially, it was very difficult. However, after the first two occasions he was amazed at the reaction of his manager. It did not lower his standing as he had feared. On the contrary, it brought them closer together. For the third quarter, he added yet another item. He would start the day by asking himself a question: What can I do today to increase the excellence of my bank? Not for his job of looking after the fixed deposits and agricultural loans, but for the bank as a whole. When he did something like helping a colleague or a client, or speaking about the bank in laudatory terms to customers, he would make a positive score. It gave him immense pleasure when he was actually able to do something. So it went on.

After about two years, he was selected for a prestigious post at his bank's branch in Hong Kong. On his way he happened to meet his teacher, who enquired about his self-development action program and his diary. He observed, "The diary has changed my life. I have acquired a lifelong friend in this little notebook that I always carry in my pocket. The first three months were the most difficult. But, as advised by you, I decided that during these three months getting rid of my habit of lying would be the most important thing in my life. I was constantly thinking of just this one goal. After the first month, when the average score fell from four to three, I felt confident that I could win. The third fortnight, when it continued to stay at three per day, was the most difficult period of the entire quarter. But, it also added to my determination to persist. Thereafter, it was a piece of cake." Prasad showed his diary for the first three months and his plans for the future to his teacher.

It is important that we have conviction and faith in this process; only then can we undertake such a challenging endeavor. If we still have doubts, then the words of Samuel Johnson should convince us of the great truth of this approach to effectiveness, quality of life and happiness:

> The foundation of content must spring up in the mind, and he who hath so little knowledge of human nature as to seek happiness by changing anything but his own disposition, will waste his life in fruitless efforts and multiply the grief he proposes to remove.[11]

Experience shows that the time required to transform a person's character depends much more on sincerity of effort than on age. Dr. Art-Ong Jumsai Na Ayudhya of Thailand, who is doing yeoman work in introducing human values in the educational system of Thailand, feels that if the intensity of effort is taken as uniform, then major transformation can take 2½ months in a 10-year-old child, in 5 months in a youth of 20, and a few years in an adult over 50. Experience with the self-development diary used by army officers suggests that those who persisted with sincerity for a period of three months experienced palpable change in themselves to a sufficient degree to continue their endeavor.

During experiments in the army, purely on a voluntary basis, a very large number of officers were enthusiasic about using a diary for self-development. However, seldom more than 15 to 20 percent of those who started persisted for a period of three months or more.* The rest dropped out. On the face of it, it was disappointing that such a large proportion of officers did not have the willpower to persist. However, it was perfectly in keeping with group behavior. Any group can be divided into three parts: one-third of the group members are positive towards their organization, one-third are neutral, and one-third are negative. If the positive

---

*Recent trials show one major reason for low results was that too many reforms were attempted simultaneously. Tackling one problem at a time gives better results.

one-third is strong enough to carry the neutral segment with them, then that organization does well and becomes effective. Organizations in which the negative one-third carries the neutral segment with them are beset with morale and discipline problems. Consequently, the 15 to 20 percent of officers who benefited from self-development endeavors were reinforcing the positive people in their units and formations. This was confirmed by formation commanders who were involved in these trials and experiments. However, the most interesting result observed in these trials, on the face of it, had no relationship to leadership.

Informal reports started coming in that those officers who persisted in maintaining a diary beyond three months not only became more effective as leaders but also became happier as individuals: "He laughs more," "He seems to be at peace," "He is far more relaxed," and "Daddy plays with us more than he ever did before" were comments about such individuals.

Equation for Happiness

It took some time before the cause of this beneficial side effect was understood. 'Pursuit of happiness' is the major goal of human life. Indeed, this goal has been enshrined almost as a fundamental right in the Constitution of the United States of America. The explanation for the happy side effect lies in the following equation for happiness, which compresses the entire wisdom of the world:

$$\text{Happiness} = \frac{\text{Number of Desires Fulfilled}}{\text{Number of Desires Entertained}}$$

To understand the equation for happiness, it is important to fully comprehend the impact of desires on human life. "Desire is the first evidence of our consciousness; we are born into sympathy and antipathy, wishing and willing."[12] As we grow, our likes and dislikes become stronger and our desire for things that we like keeps on increasing. We get deluded into believing that things satisfying our senses will give us happiness. We seek music we

120

like that satisfies our ears, smooth and soft things that yield pleasure to our skin, things of beauty that appeal to our eyes, food and drink that are tasty to the tongue, fragrance that appeals to the nose, and wealth, property, name, recognition, status and power that we feel will make our mind happy. The truth is that uncontrolled desires "fog the intellect, pervert vision; desires create a mirage where there was none before; they clothe things with desirability. To escape from the clutches of desires—which give birth to the brood of anger, malice, greed, envy, falsehood etc.—one has to cleanse one's consciousness."[13]

Frustration caused by nonfulfillment of desires leads to anger and then to its linked subsidiaries—hate and jealousy—which blind us. Desire that is fulfilled does give temporary satisfaction, but it also multiplies itself manifold, and that makes us greedy and burn with envy. Uncontrolled desires, consequently, are the source of all the unhappiness, agitation, drug addiction, crime, violence, fractured relations and divorce that are hounding most of the societies in the world. Cumulatively, desires for worldly things make us extremely selfish, as depicted in figure 7.1.

The twentieth century can well be designated as the century of advertising on radio and television. Images are carried "through the realm of fantasy, knowledge and feeling to the ego's central core of wish and desire. It [desire] extends and intensifies cravings"[14]—cravings related particularly to carnal pleasures and possessive greed. And craving" is the principal cause of suffering and wrongdoing, and the greatest obstacle between the human soul and its divine Ground."[15]

Keeping up with the Joneses is the mental cancer that leads to numerous desires that have absolutely no relation to the needs of an individual or a family. It merely gives rise to wants, and wants can be endless. Endless is the pain and agitation that they eventually bring in their wake.

The equation for happiness suggests that if we have the willpower to control our desires and keep them limited, then our happiness quotient goes up - the lesser the denominator - the number of desires entertained - the higher will be our peace of mind and happiness.

Experiences of scientists of the soul throughout the world are that "Desirelessness is the condition of deliverance and illumination."[16]

If all the pleasures in the world are equal to one unit,* then the joy, happiness and bliss which is within each human being and can be experienced by renouncing desires is equal to 10 units[22]. —Taitteriya Upanishad II, Stanza 8

Once we acquire the strength of mind to control and limit our desires and start moving towards this goal, our joy and happiness keeps on increasing—control is not achieved by suppression of desires, but by discrimination and intelligent evaluation of good and bad, of right and wrong, and of short-term satisfaction versus long-term misery and, above all, by dispassionate judgment in separating wants from needs. It would be appropriate to look at what some spiritual scientists have said about desires, wishing and asking:

It was from the Nameless that Heaven and Earth sprang;
The named is but the mother that rears
    the ten thousand creatures, each after its kind.

---

*"A human being enjoys one unit of worldly pleasures when he is young, well educated, well disciplined, mentally resolute, physically strong, comes to possess the whole world's riches and its joys."

NETWORK OF SELFISHNESS

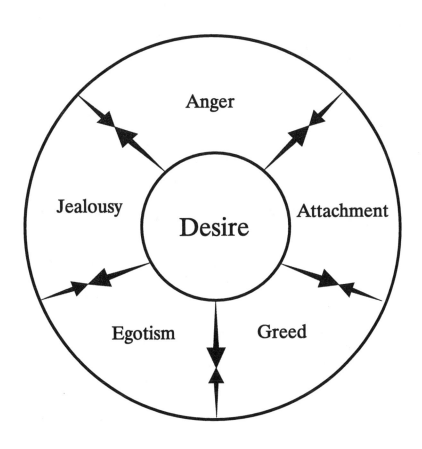

Figure 7.1

Truly, "only he that rids himself of desire can see
  the Secret Essence."
He that has never rid himself of desire can
  only see the Outcomes.   —Lao-Tzu

0 Lord, I, a beggar, ask of Thee more than a
thousand kings may ask of Thee. Each one has
something he needs to ask of Thee; I have come to
ask Thee to give me Thyself.   —Ansari of Heart

The Savor of wandering in the ocean of deathless
  life has rid me of all my asking;
As tree is in seed, so all disease is in asking.   —Kabir

I have hardly any desires, but if I were to be born again, I
should have none at all. We should ask nothing and refuse
nothing, but leave ourselves in the arms of the Divine
Providence without wasting time in any desire, except to will
what God wills of us.   —St. Fancois de Sales

Desire leads to hatred of those who thwart it, fondness for
those who feed it and the inevitable wheel of likes and
dislikes.   —Sai Baba

In the mind lake of man there lurks a poisonous serpent—
desire. When that is destroyed, the various frailties and
frivolities; triumphs, trials and failures; and pain and pleasure
the desire brings in its train surrender to God. —Sai Baba

Place a ceiling on desires and be happy.   —Sai Baba

Less luggage, more comfort, easy journey (by train and in
life).   —Sai Baba

The Indian Army experiments that drew our attention to the side effect of increased happiness among those who persisted in the task of self-development has an obvious lesson. If we have the determination, and persist in achieving a simple goal in the challenging endeavor of self-development, we also will acquire the willpower to control desires. That is why willpower has been designated as the king of virtues in a leader. As our desires change from personal worldly wants to higher ideals and accomplishments, we ascend in our effectiveness as leaders and in happiness, as shown in figure 7.2.

We have discussed two major techniques that can help in transforming our character. Best results are achieved when both are combined. When we decide to change a habit or acquire one, and then persist till we win a victory, then it enormously reinforces our confidence to go on. It is wise to choose simpler goals for the first three months, and then add on more difficult ones as our tenacity becomes stronger. In chapter 8 we shall discuss how we can be motivated to persist. It is in this area that reading about the lives of outstanding leaders helps a great deal.

When we read about the lives of leaders who developed their potential by self-effort, we get enormous inspiration to stay the course.

Note for Teachers

Obviously, this is the most important chapter of the book. Students have to be inspired to undertake an action program to improve themselves. The steps showing how this might be undertaken have been outlined. However, it often requires one-to-one counseling with patience and love to motivate an individual. "What if I fail?" is a fear often expressed when people learn that they can indeed improve themselves. If the targets chosen for the first endeavor are modest, then the chances of failure are

THE ASCENT OF MAN

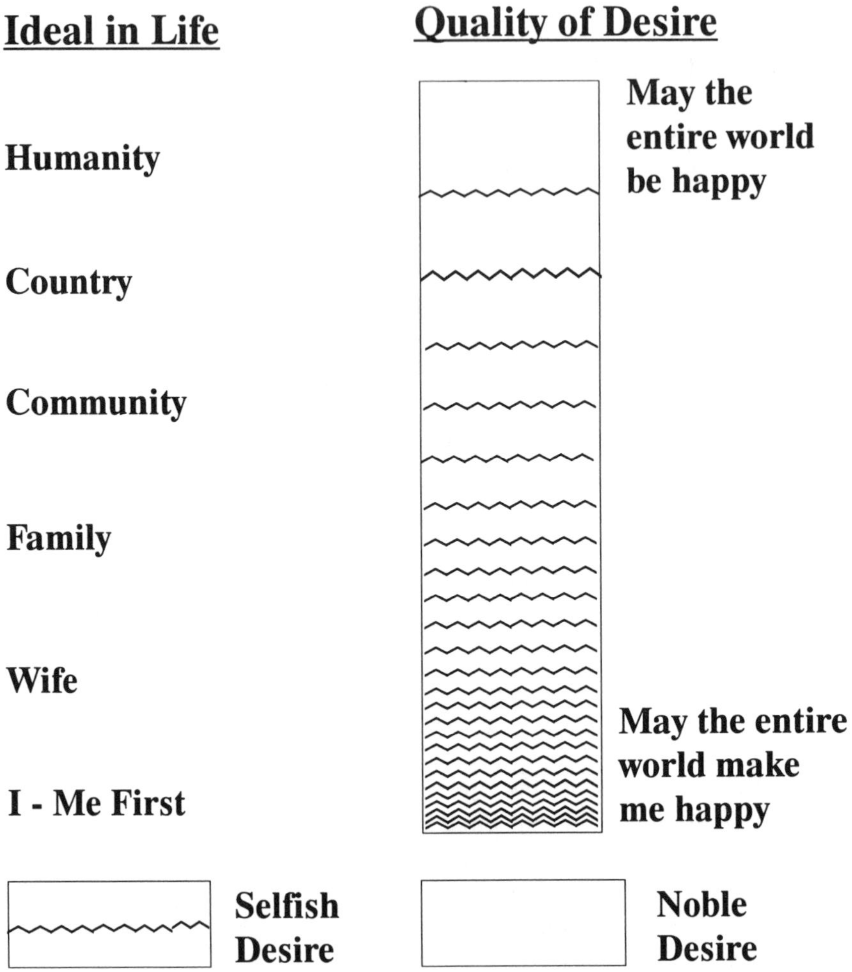

Ideal in Life

Humanity

Country

Community

Family

Wife

I - Me First

Quality of Desire

May the entire world be happy

May the entire world make me happy

Selfish Desire

Noble Desire

Figure 7.2

comparatively small. Some examples of the simpler targets that may help individuals gain self-confidence come from Britain. There the technique of maintaining a self-improvement diary has been successfully used in many public schools (meaning private residential schools). Given below are some of the goals chosen for changing or acquiring habits:

- I will not lick my fingers at the dining table.

- I will brush my teeth in the morning and after dinner.

- I won't pick my nose.

- I shall arrange my books before going to sleep.

- I will write one page of good handwriting every day.

- I will recite my prayer sitting in the bed before hitting the pillow.

- I will not report it when a senior punishes me.

Among young adults, targets like giving up smoking, candy, coffee, etc.; losing 10 lbs; running a mile in 4.8 minutes or whatever; and giving up daydreaming have been found useful. Some individuals wish to eradicate weaknesses that are so personal and private they don't wish to disclose them to anyone, and certainly not reduce them to writing in a diary. They may be advised to use a code in such a situation.

Controlling desires promotes a very interesting and often animated discussion. Students should be encouraged to contribute their personal experiences of desiring things, facilities or situations that are clearly wants aroused by advertising, peer pressure or prompting of the senses. It is useful to come prepared for discussion.

Some students need a little mathematical help to understand the equation. This should be given.

Elimination of all desires, at times, provokes heated controversy between those who are spiritually aware and those who are totally worldly. In such a situation, attention should be drawn to the pragmatic advice given about placing a "ceiling on desires." We should entertain only as many desires as we have the capability to fulfill. The moment we go beyond our capacity, we are bound to create problems for ourselves and others.

Giving follow-up encouragement to students who decide to make a start is the most sacred duty of a teacher. It should be done discreetly, unobtrusively and without pushing.

8
Sustaining Motivation for Self-development to be a Leader

We have discussed how everyone wants to improve, but only a few persist in their efforts. How can we overcome this inertia?

It is a universal experience that resistance to changing habits of thought, word and deed developed over a long time is extremely strong. It is like the tremendous gravity pull experienced by space vehicles that have to break out of the Earth's gravity to go into space. In doing so, more energy is "spent in the first few minutes of lift off, and the first few miles of travel"[1] than is required during the rest of the journey, for the days on end and millions of miles spent in reaching the moon and other planets. The same is the case when we want to break away from deeply embedded habits like selfishness, procrastination, lack of perseverance, dishonesty etc., which are serious impediments to effective leadership. To succeed in breaking away "involves more than a little willpower and a few minor changes in our lives. 'Lift off' takes tremendous effort, but once we break out of the gravity pull, our freedom takes on a whole new dimension."[2] It is because of this great difficulty that thinkers and savants like Patanjali in ancient India have advised that transformation needs determined effort "over a long time,"—so that we can alter the very course of our lives and become masters of our destiny. In order to change our habits it is important that:

CHANGING HABITS

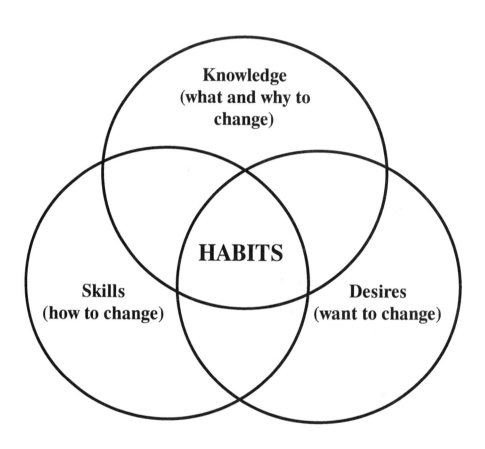

Figure 8.1

- We understand why do we want to change them, and what new habits we should acquire. This knowledge comes from awareness of our strengths and weaknesses in relation to the universal inner structure of good leaders.

- We have the desire to change. This desire grows out of an ideal or a vision we have in life and the need to become more effective to fulfil our ideal or vision. Desire to change also grows from an awareness that success in self-development and improving our character leads to happiness in life (this was discussed in chapter 7).

- We know how to go about changing our habits. We have already discussed the time-tested technique of reading about the lives of outstanding world leaders and the instrument called the self-development diary.

In a nutshell, success in changing habits depends on interaction and balance of the above three factors,[3] which are diagrammatically illustrated on page 133.

Once we are clear in our mind what, why and how we want to transform, we have to develop an action program that will lead us to our goal. If we want to be masters of our destiny by transforming our character, we must invest substantially in the main instrument that will give us this mastery—ourselves. The main investment needed has also been tested over and over again in human history in all societies and cultures round the world. The essential inputs for this transformation are:

- Time

- Willpower to persist

The experience of transforming human nature suggests that balanced investment of time and willpower in a few activities keeps a person motivated to persist in transforming himself or herself. Incessant industrious work is the secret of success, remembering all the time that "all true work is rest,"[4] and indeed "change of work is leisure."[5] The essential investments are:

Investment in the Health of the Body. Only a healthy body that can endure hard physical and mental work can contribute to rapid transformation, indeed, success in any venture. About 45 minutes a day devoted to exercise are most essential. Yogic exercises developed in India are excellent for improving the health of the body and mind. However, walking, jogging, swimming, working out in a gymnasium, and so on are also good. Eating food that is pure, and prepared with love is essential too. Most of our illnesses are caused by eating the wrong types of food, overindulgence and lack of exercise. It is now very well established that reducing our intake of food to about 70 percent of what is considered normal contributes to good health, clarity of mind and longevity.

Investment in the Health of the Mind. "Extraordinary powers are in the mind of man"[6] sums up the Indian experience of the potential of every person; thoughts, emotions, memory, imagination and discrimination are all functions of the mind. Just as the face and voice of one person differs from another, so also his or her mental world, mode of thinking, way of understanding things, and reaction to events differs. Consequently, in the Indian experience of human transformation, great emphasis is laid on the purity, health and control of the mind. Meditation and reading are time-tested techniques that keep the mind alert, vigorous, stimulated and positive. Reading classics and books on great lives, our field of work, leadership and spirituality should form part of our daily routine. The aim of everyone who aspires to soar high should be to read about 18 books a year, the average for the most successful people.

Investment in Spiritual Health. Emphasis on spiritual growth in the process of transformation is a major part of human heritage. Its importance for leadership effectiveness is now finding recognition in the West also. Self-help author Stephen Covey, while recommending meditation, observes that the "spiritual dimension is your core, your center, your commitment to your value system. It is a very private area of life and a supremely important one. It draws upon the sources that inspire and uplift you and tie you to the timeless truths of all humanity."[7] It is through meditation for 20 to 30 minutes a day that we can contemplate over the timeless and also can understand the eternal questions Who am I? What is the purpose of life? and What is the secret of enduring bliss?, thus awakening the hidden divinity present in each one of us so we can rise above religions marked by ceremony. "It is good to be born in a religion, but it is not good to die in one. Grow and rescue yourself from the limits and regulations and doctrines that fence in your freedom of thought, the ceremonies and rites that restrict and direct. Reach the point where churches do not matter, where all roads end from where all roads begin."[8] This investment is the most productive in inspiring us to supreme efforts.

Investment in the Health of Society. Seva (service) to our fellow human beings, not for reward or recognition, but for its own sake is the most exhilarating experience in our lives. "Hands that serve are holier than the lips that pray."[9] And yet we are reluctant to undertake service activities. The pleasure that we derive from anonymous service is far beyond any other source of joy, and yet most of us shy away from it. For the transformation of our character, service without any selfish motive gives us potent inspiration to persist. It is so because "service broadens your vision, widens your awareness, deepens your compassion."[10] That is also the reason why service is a key activity needed for effective leadership. "If one who understands the spirit of service becomes a leader, that leader will always retain and enjoy his leadership through service. Without understanding service and first becoming a leader servant, one cannot become a leader."[11] The Indian ethos in this field is summed up by the Sanskrit word *Paropakara*, which means, and enjoins citizens to, "live for others." Dr. Hans Selye,

133

in his monumental work on stress, concludes that "a long, healthy and happy life is the result of making contributions, of having meaningful projects that are personally exciting and contribute to and bless the lives of others."[12] George Bernard Shaw concludes the same thing when he says, "This is the true joy in life—that being used for a purpose recognized by yourself as a mighty one. That being a force of nature instead of feverish, selfish little clod of ailments and grievances complaining that the world will not devote itself to making you happy. I am of the opinion that my life belongs to the whole community, and as long as I live, it is my privilege to do for it, whatever I can.[13] Our aim every day should be to "at least serve one other human being by making deposits of unconditional love."[14] We can then be rays of sunshine and harbingers of joy and hope. Each day will then be a day of our own growth and transformation as well.

If we invest in our transformation, using the time-tested measures we have discussed, then we shall acquire lifelong inspiration to grow and become the masters of our destiny.

We have discussed the methodology of maintaining a self-development diary in chapter 7. We have also discussed the great value of reading about the lives of outstanding individuals who continue to inspire humanity. The best results are achieved when we adopt both techniques simultaneously.

Not all the 108 lives listed at the end of the book will excite every individual. However, when we read, say, 10 books or so, we do come across a few people that trigger some latent forces in our subconscious mind and inspire us to emulate them. We should start studying books on such people in depth.

Out of the 108 lives, brief life sketches of three are included in this chapter—three who in recent times have inspired a vast number of people in the world. There are other reasons as well for their inclusion. All of them are excellent examples of individuals who transformed their character by self-effort. They belong to three different continents. Each is from a totally different strata of society—working class, middle class and aristocracy. All of them had a deep faith in the Supreme Creator. And finally all three had a vision of the world becoming a large well-integrated global state. They are:

- Benjamin Franklin of the United States (born in 1706)

- Mahatma Gandhi of India (born in 1869)

- Winston Spencer Churchill of Great Britain (born in 1874)

Benjamin Franklin, as the representative of the British colonies in North America, tried to persuade the ministers in Great Britain to grant "home rule" to the American colonies. In this samaritan step, the American visionary saw the potential for a permanent linkage between Great Britain and America in a grand world federation. British ministers flatly refused, and the American colonies revolted and broke away. About 150 years later, Mahatma Gandhi similarly tried to persuade British ministers to grant independence to India as a move towards the world becoming one large human family. Winston Churchill vehemently opposed this proposal. Churchill also had a vision of the world, but he saw it as unified under the tutelage of the British aristocracy. As we move into the twenty-first century, the world is inexorably moving towards the unity of humankind. Consequently, these three men should be of special interest and inspiration to the leaders of tomorrow. Study the three lives and vast horizons will open up to you.

The brief life sketches of Benjamin Franklin, Mahatma Gandhi and Winston Churchill given in this chapter are merely introductory in nature. So vast and varied are their achievements that it is not possible to do justice to their contribution to mankind in just a few pages. These sketches focus on their early lives, so as to inspire youth's understanding that *it is* possible to become masters of our destiny, if we make the necessary effort.

While reading about these three inspirational lives, we should try to understand how the character of the individuals was molded to make them what they were. Among many outstanding leaders in history, we find the influence of a teacher, a guide or a guru who transformed them into what Plato called a "philosopher king," as can be seen in the examples below:

Leader	Was Influenced By
Alexander the Great of Macedonia	Aristotle
Chandragupta Maurya of India	Chanakya
Shivaji of India	Sage Samarth Ramdas

Sage Vidyaranya, who inspired the forging of the mighty Vijayanagar empire in South India, articulated the concept advocated by Bhishma (see introduction) and Plato of the "philosopher king," in a beautiful Sanskrit verse:

I Charitum Shakyum Samyagrajyadhi Loukikam.

(Only a man of steady character and wisdom can carry out the task of leading and administering a kingdom effectively.)

Benjamin Franklin

The life of Benjamin Franklin, one of the most respected founding fathers of the USA, is, perhaps, the finest example in history of a self-made man. How did this young man, born in relative poverty and denied formal schooling, transform himself into a flourishing businessman, a diplomat, a cosmopolitan savant, an inventor and a citizen of the world?

136

His public career took him to London as the chief spokesman of the British colonies in North America. Unfortunately, British statesmen did not possess the wisdom of Benjamin Franklin. They wanted to rule their colonies directly from London, instead of granting them self-government, as suggested by Franklin. The impasse led to the colonies writing the Declaration of Independence. After this seditious document was signed, Benjamin Franklin, retaining his sense of humor, quipped, "We must all hang together, or assuredly we shall hang separately." Soon the American Revolution broke out. Franklin was selected to garner foreign support for the war and was sent to France—then the enemy of Great Britain. He successfully secured enough financial and military help to effectively fight the British. This happened just a few years earlier than the French Revolution in 1789. Franklin had many admirers in England, where he was eventually able to negotiate a treaty with Great Britain that recognized the former Thirteen Colonies in America as sovereign states. Finally, he played an active role in framing the American Constitution. It was he who proposed that, despite differences of opinion among delegates, the Constitution should be adopted unanimously. Such was Franklin's stature that his plea was accepted.

His story has inspired thousands of youth to improve themselves by using industry, frugality and willpower to change their character for the better. Our aim in studying the life of Benjamin Franklin should be to learn how this boy from an ordinary working-class family improved and transformed himself so that "all his activities, all his inventions, all his works in philosophy, economics, politics and science were directed to one end—the benefit of mankind."[15] In the process of improving himself, he improved everything that he touched.

Benjamin's parents, dyers by trade, emigrated from Great Britain to the USA in 1682. They left their home to escape the religious bigotry that prevailed then. Benjamin, born in January 1706, was the youngest son. He showed promise at letters and was sent to school, where he soon made his mark as a bright student. However, his father could not afford the cost of schooling and also did not like the "mean living many so educated were afterwards able to obtain."[16] So, after about two years, he was withdrawn from school in favor of being trained as an artisan in one trade or the other.

For a while, Benjamin assisted his father in his soap and candle-making business. But he did not like this occupation. He had a large group of playmates who accepted his leadership in difficult situations. Among various games and activities they enjoyed was fishing in a marsh near the sea. To escape having to stand in the marsh for hours, they decided to build a platform. Guided by Benjamin, the boys stole a number of cut stones from a building under construction and put together a decent platform. Before long the missing stones were traced to the boys. They were, quite naturally, taken to task by their parents. Benjamin argued at length with his father about the platform's usefulness for their fishing. But his father was able to convince him that "nothing was useful which was not honest."[17] (Honesty means not lying, stealing or cheating.) This incident gave Benjamin the foundation for his character.

Around the age of 12, he was made an apprentice under his elder brother James, who, having learned the trade of printing, had just set up his own printing press. Benjamin welcomed this opportunity, as it put him in direct touch with the world of books and newspapers. He was already borrowing and buying books, and in his apprenticeship he saw a great opportunity to educate himself. He plunged into devouring books with greater intensity, devoting many hours to reading before and after work at the press. When a friend working in a book shop managed to smuggle out a good book for him to read, he would stay up the whole night to finish it. He was careful to keep it clean and place it back in the shop early in the morning.

Among numerous classics, historic and other seminal works that Benjamin read, he was deeply influenced by Dr. Mather's *Essays to Do Good*. It had an influence on "some of the principal future events of my life."[18] For a while he tried his hand at poetry but was firmly guided by his father to give it up because "verse makers were generally beggars!"[19]

Around the age of sixteen, Franklin turned vegetarian after reading about its benefits in a book. He found that it was much cheaper and that it also accelerated his studies "from that greater clearness of head and quicker comprehension which usually attend temperance in eating."[20] He found that bread, a handful of raisins and a glass of water made an excellent meal! (He did not remain a strict vegetarian for long.)

He also started reading all that was available about Socrates. From this he learned the art of persuading others to accept your point of view. Abrupt contradiction and strong argument antagonizes the other person. "An air of humble inquirer and doubter ... expressed with modest diffidence"[21] has a better chance of success. Words like *certainly* and *undoubtedly* give an air of positiveness of opinion and are disputed. Words like "I conceive or apprehend so and so; it appears to me; I should think it to be so, or it is so, if I am not mistaken"[22] have a far better chance of persuading others. Benjamin goes on to remind us of Pope's words:

Men should be taught as if you taught them not.
And things unknown proposed as things forgot.

Later in his youth, he was to learn another lesson about persuading people. He realized the "impropriety of presenting oneself as the proposer of any useful project that might be supposed to raise one's reputation in the smallest degree above that of one's neighbor."[23] It is best to push such ideas on behalf of others or an institution. He soon learned that "the present little

139

sacrifice of your vanity will afterwards be amply rewarded."[24] Franklin applied this lesson in his life with great success. This is the truth Lao-tzu had taught more than 2,000 years ago: "True self-interest [of a leader] teaches selflessness." However, before Franklin could fully learn this lesson, he started having trouble with his brother. James, being much older, would not desist from thrashing him, when, Benjamin records on reflection, "perhaps I was too saucy and provoking."[25] He decided to leave his brother and secretly moved away to New York. Not finding any work there, he drifted to Philadelphia, where he got work at a press. With his diligence and learning, he soon made a name for himself in the town as a promising young man. The governor, Sir William Keith, started taking interest in him and encouraged him to set up a press of his own. He even offered to give him letters of credit to procure the necessary machinery from London.

Benjamin sailed to London. After disembarking there, he found that the governor had deceived him; there were no letters of credit for him. From one Mr. Denham, whom he had befriended during the voyage, he learned that the governor was a good man but "liberal of promises which he never meant to keep."[26] Unfortunately, he had acquired a bad habit: "He wished to please every body; and having little to give he gave expectations."[27] People who do not do what they say are soon found out and then no one trusts them. Benjamin at the age of 18 learned never to behave like that.

He stayed in London for about 18 months by working at leading presses in the city. He was known as Water America among his coworkers for refusing to drink beer! But he acquired great experience in the trade and made some very fine friends in the field of learning and letters. He kept in touch with Denham and learned a major lesson from this trader.

Denham had escaped to America when his business in Bristol, England, failed and he could not pay his creditors. After sincere, hard work for a few years, he had returned to England as a man of some fortune. Soon after reaching England, he invited all his old creditors to a banquet. Before dinner started, he made a short speech thanking them all for bearing with him. Then the formal dinner started, and all the invitees thought that a good meal was the only thing they would get out of Denham. But when the plates of the first course were removed, everyone found under his plate "an order on a bank for the full amount of the unpaid remainder with interest."[29] To young Benjamin it was an example of honest and right conduct that he sought to emulate in his life.

He returned to the USA in the employment of Denham's trading company and learned how to run a good business. Within six months, Denham died, and Benjamin went back into printing work. Within two years, he was able to set up his own press. By this time he had been fully convinced that "truth, sincerity and integrity in dealings between man and man were of utmost importance for felicity in life."[29]

At about this time he started a small club, limited to 12 members for their mutual improvement. He called it the Junto Club. Every Friday they met and discussed matters pertaining to morals, politics and philosophy. They also wrote essays once in three months. Members of the club included a mathematician, a surveyor, a shoemaker, a joiner, a gentleman of fortune and a clerk. Reading and learning was their common interest. Most of the ideas and projects that Benjamin implemented in his life came out of these discussions.

His hard and honest work gave his business activities character and credit. His printing press flourished. Business started pouring in.

In 1732, he first published his *Poor Richard's Almanack* under the pen name of Richard Saunders. It became a best-seller. For 25 years, it gave him both fortune and a vehicle to market

141

morality. He would fill up the almanack with proverbs and sayings that contained wisdom of many ages and nations. It was translated and printed widely throughout Europe.

As his business flourished, he took up many public projects, starting institutions that now are considered standard in any town in the USA—a library, a fire company, an insurance company and a hospital. He set up an academy that today is the University of Pennsylvania, one of the finest institutions of higher learning in USA. His interest in things scientific was equally significant. He invented a stove for heating rooms; the lightning conductor, which is now a standard fixture on buildings around the world; and bifocal glasses for those with weak eyesight. Designating electric current as positive and negative was also his gift.

At about the age of 24, Benjamin married Ms. Reid. She had seen him on the first day of his arrival in Philadelphia, about seven years earlier. He was dirty, dishevelled and hungry after the arduous journey from New York. He had bought three large rolls of bread and walked the streets carrying a roll under each arm and eating the third one. She thought he "made a most awkward and ridiculous appearance."[30] She was a good wife to him as long as she lived and shared his frugality and industry. "My breakfast was for a long time bread and milk (no tea) and I ate it out of a two penny earthen porringer with a pewter spoon. But mark how luxury enters families in spite of principle. One morning I found my breakfast in a china bowl with a silver spoon .... My wife bought it because she thought her husband deserved a silver spoon and china bowl as well as any of his neighbors."[31]

Perhaps, Franklin's greatest gift to humanity is the few pages of his autobiography where he explains how a diary helped him to develop virtues that he thought he needed. At about the time he was married, he conceived "the bold and arduous project of arriving at moral perfection."[32] He reflected on his character and picked out 13 virtues in which he felt he needed to change his habits to become perfect. These, along with his explanation of each, were:

1. *Temperance.*   Eat not to dullness, drink not to elevation.

2. *Silence.*   Speak not, but what may benefit others or yourself; avoid trifling conversations.

3. *Order.*   Let all things have their places, let each part of your business have its time.

4. *Resolution.*   Resolve to perform what you ought; perform without fail what you resolve.

5. *Frugality.*   Make no expense, but to do good to others or yourself, i.e., waste nothing.

6. *Industry.*   Lose no time; be always employed in something useful; cut off all unnecessary action.

7. *Sincerity.*   Use no hurtful deceit; think innocently and justly; and if you speak, speak accordingly.

8. *Justice.*   Wrong none by doing injustice, or omitting the benefit that are your duty.

9. *Moderation.*   Avoid extremes; forbear resenting injuries so much as you think they deserve.

10. *Cleanliness.*   Tolerate no uncleanliness in body, clothes or habitation.

11. *Tranquility.*   Be not disturbed at trifles, or at accidents common or unavoidable.

12. *Chastity.*   [Did not elaborate.]

13. *Humility.*   Imitate Jesus and Socrates.

To achieve perfection in all the virtues, he decided to concentrate on one at a time for a full week. After mastering it, he would go on to the next one for a week, thus taking 13 weeks to complete one cycle and doing four cycles in a year.

He made a small notebook containing a page prepared for each virtue, as shown in figure 8.2. There are 7 columns for the 7 days

TEMPERANCE							
EAT NOT TO DULLNESS DRINK NOT TO ELEVATION							
	S	M	T	W	T	F	S
T							
S	*	*		*		*	
O	**	*	*		*	*	*
R		*				*	
F		*		*			
I		*					
S							
J							
M							
C							
T							
C							
H							

Figure 8.2. Form of the Pages.

of the week. And there are 13 lines—one for each of the 13 virtues. The first capital letter of the virtue was written on its lines.

Franklin made a mark with a black pencil whenever he committed a fault in a virtue on a particular day. He did this every evening after reflection on the whole day. Over a period of 13 weeks, he gave strict attention to each virtue successively. Thus, during the first week, he concentrated on avoiding the least deviation from temperance. He left the other virtues to their chance and only marked every evening the faults of the day. Such concentrated attention kept the temperance line spotless throughout the week and brought that habit under sufficient control.

He shifted to the second habit in the next week and tried to keep that line spotless also. He explains that the process was like weeding a vegetable garden. You cannot weed the whole garden in one go. You weed one bed at a time. On weeding the 13th bed, you come back to the first one again. By this repetitive but concentrated process, it was slowly possible to see the pages of the book staying spotless. He would rub off the spots after each cycle, but that made his notebook smudgy. So after a few years, he changed over to an ivory notebook, which could quite easily be wiped clean. Over the years, he found his faults diminishing. In later years, he repeated the cycle once a year, or once in two years. He regretted to record that he could never fully master order, thus wasting a lot of time searching for things that he had not kept in the designated place.

On one page of the notebook he had charted out the program for a normal day, allotting time to various activities. He started the day by deciding on the day's resolution and what good he was going to do during the day. Similarly, he fixed time for reflection on the day's activities.

Wisdom and virtue among leaders at the family or national level have resulted in civilizations, reaching their golden age. The lack of these qualities has brought them decline and deprivation. The rise of the USA was to a large measure due to leaders like Benjamin Franklin, who laid the foundation of that nation about 200 years ago. Franklin's life is proof of "how little necessary all origin is to happiness, virtue and greatness,"[33] wrote a friend of Franklin, who persuaded him to complete his autobiography.

It is in our youth that we should read the autobiography of Benjamin Franklin—in youth, because it is then that we plant our chief habits and prejudices, that we decide on our profession, pursuits and matrimony.

Mahatma Gandhi

"Many leaders have moved across the modern world stage with much more spectacular flourish and greater aplomb than Mahatma Gandhi. Few have wielded an influence so momentous and so revolutionary on the history of our times."[34] Gandhi galvanized the Indian people to wage a war without violence— Satyagraha—to win their independence. Victory in that mighty undertaking was the beginning of the end for imperialism and colonialism in the world, restoring resources of the Earth to their rightful owners. Gandhi's struggle and success have made a major contribution to accelerating humanity's movement towards a new age—an age of the Unity of Man, Global Economy and Earth Citizenship.

How did Gandhi, a shy introverted boy develop into a leader who occupies a place in the very forefront of the top one hundred great lives of all ages and arenas of human endeavor? And this happened in spite of his being cowardly as a schoolboy, as Gandhi later recollected, "I used to be haunted by the fear of thieves, ghosts and serpents. I did not dare stir out of doors at night."[35] He was afraid to sleep without a light in his bedroom and felt ashamed of himself because even his wife had more courage than him.

On January 30, 1948, the same person, at the age of 78, was walking in New Delhi to join worshippers for the normal evening prayer. There was a crowd of about a thousand people. As Gandhi approached the seated crowd, a man got up from the front row and moved towards the slow-moving Mahatma as if to pay him homage. The man moved within two feet of Gandhi, then whipped out a pistol and fired three shots. Gandhi died on the spot, and the whole world was plunged into mourning.

Spontaneous homage was paid to this "private citizen without wealth, property, official title, official post, academic distinction, scientific achievement or artistic gift."[36] Nearly 3,450 messages of sympathy poured in from countries outside India. Leon Blum, the French socialist articulated what millions round the world felt. He wrote. "I never saw Gandhi; I do not know his language. I never set foot in his country, and yet I feel the same sorrow as if I had lost someone near and dear. The whole world has been plunged into mourning by the death of this extraordinary man."[37] Albert Einstein asserted that "a powerful human following can be assembled not only through the cunning game of the usual political maneuvers and trickeries, but through the cogent example of a morally superior conduct of life. In our time of utter moral decadence he was the only statesman to stand for higher human relationship in the political sphere." [38] General Douglas MacArthur of the USA was the supreme allied commander of the occupation forces in Japan after World War II. This great hero and intellectual of the two world wars, who spent his life in the profession devoted to the "management of violence," wrote about Gandhi's faith in nonviolence in these words: "In the evolution of civilization, if it is to survive, all men cannot fail eventually to adopt Gandhi's belief that the process of man's application of force to resolve contentious issues is fundamentally not only wrong, but contains within itself the germs of self-destruction."[39] This is a great historical analysis and truth about the use of armed might in the affairs of humankind.

The story of Gandhi's transformation through self-effort is a fascinating one. A path available to any one of us, *provided* we are willing to make the effort. The path that shows there can be no lasting achievement in life if the means employed to get it are not in keeping with human values. Therefore, to *live* based on these values is the royal road not only to enduring excellence in any field but also to happiness, peace and contentment in life.

Gandhi was born on October 2, 1869 in well-to-do business caste family of grocers (*Gandhi* means "grocer"). However, for two generations the family had been the dewans (chief administrators) of a few miniature princely states in Gujarat, in the western part of India. Gandhi's father, Karamchand, "had no education save that of experience. But he was incorruptible and had earned a reputation for strict impartiality in his family as well as outside."[40] He was known for his loyalty and moral courage in upholding the interests of the rulers he served.

Mohandas Karamchand Gandhi was the fourth and last son of his father's fourth wife; Karamchand had married four times in succession.

Young Mohandas was very fond of his mother Puttlibai. He was much influenced by this pious and saintly lady. She never ate a meal without saying her prayers and visited the community temple every day. She was used to long fasts and liberally undertook vows, which she observed with tenacity. During the Chaturmas, a four-month period of fasting during the rainy season, she habitually lived on one meal. And even during this period, she would undertake a variety of vows. Sometimes, it would be full fast every alternate day. At other times, she would eat only after she could see the sun. The children would wait for the sun to show up through the clouds and run to her when it peeped out. Occasionally, by the time she came out to see the sun herself it was again covered by clouds. She would tell the children not to worry because "the Creator does not want me to eat today"[41] and would go about her housekeeping chores with perfect equanimity.

During one Chaturmas she vowed to eat her meal only after a koel (a singing black bird known for cooing with joy during the rainy season) had cooed. Gandhi loved his mother dearly and did not want her to miss her meals. So one day, when the bird did not coo for a long time, he went out and imitated the voice of the bird. Then came rushing in and told his mother that the koel had cooed and she should eat her meal. Puttlibai had seen through his prank. She held the young lad by the hand and gave him two tight slaps. She advised him never to tell a lie again no matter what happened. This simple act by a loving mother who was a living example of firm adherence to her principles made a deep impact on Gandhi's mind. *Truth* became the foundation of his character.[42]

When Gandhi started his studies in the local school, he was, according to his own account, a mediocre student. Being shy and reticent, he did not mix very much with other boys. The moment school was over, he would literally run back home. But he was a stickler for punctuality even at that young age. Once the school was visited by the education inspector, Mr. Giles. By then Gandhi was 12 years old. The students in his class were asked by the inspector to spell five English words. Gandhi misspelled the word *kettle*. The regular teacher, who was pacing up and down the aisle, noticed the mistake. He desperately tried hinting to Gandhi to copy the right spelling from his neighbor's slate. Gandhi refused. Later the teacher scolded him for his stupidity, which had spoiled the record of the class, since all the other boys had gotten the spellings right. Gandhi had deep respect for his teacher, but it did not include cheating at his behest. This experience became another landmark in the development of Gandhi's character, later to be remembered with joy.

Gandhi was married at the age of 13 in accordance with the then prevailing custom in Gujarat. Later he spoke out against the "wretched practice" of child marriage in his writings. He felt that it arrested the growth of Indians, keeping them from reaching their full potential.

Being conscious of his cowardly nature, Gandhi was much impressed by a small Gujarati poem, which in those days was making the rounds among schoolboys:

> Behold the mighty Englishman;
> He rules the Indians small;
> Because being a meat eater
> He is five cubits tall.[43]

The vegetarian Gujarati boys felt that if the Indians ate meat, they could expel the British from India. He was persuaded by a close school friend, Sheikh Mehboob, to try eating meat. Secretly, when away from his family, who were strict vegetarians, he did try it. Despite the disagreeable reaction to it, he persisted in the experiment once or twice a week as a patriotic duty! However, he was most uncomfortable about not telling his parents the truth. Finally, he gave up the experiment; since he could not bear the strain of falsehood and deceit.

At about the age of 15, Gandhi stole a small piece of gold from his brother's armlet. This produced a moral crisis in Gandhi's mind. He wanted to tell the truth to his father so he could cleanse himself. Finally, he wrote the details in Gujarati and ended his confession by saying that he would never steal again and requesting his father's forgiveness. He silently passed on the letter to his sick father, whose legs Gandhi used to press every evening till the old dewan fell asleep. His father sat up in bed and just cried. Gandhi sat near him and also wept. No words were spoken. None were necessary. Tears of love said what had to be said. The incident greatly reinforced Gandhi's moral fiber. His father died a few months later in 1885.

Gandhi graduated from high school but could not settle down in a college. His father's wish was that he should become a lawyer and then take up the family tradition of working one's way up to become the chief administrator of one of the miniature princely states. In those days the shortest route to becoming a lawyer was to go to England for a three-year course. Gandhi was very keen to go, but there were hurdles. His mother did not want to send her youngest son away. At the same time, he had no money. For a while, in his eagerness to go to England, he toyed with the idea of pawning his wife's jewelry. However, the matter was finally settled when his elder brother, a lawyer, undertook to provide the financial support. His mother also agreed to let him go after the family guru made him vow that during his stay in London he would not "touch wine, women and meat."[44] But then there arose a last-minute hitch. The elders of Gandhi's caste heard of his proposed visit to England for studies. They met in Bombay and summoned Gandhi. There they advised him to give up his plan, since they felt that he would not be able to practice his religion properly in England. Gandhi refused. Then they passed a resolution declaring him an outcaste!

Gandhi reached London in 1888 at the age of 21 and spent two years and eight months in England. He studied law in the Inner Temple—the most aristocratic of the four institutions preparing students for the courts. For a while he tried to do what he later called, "ape the English gentleman." He dressed as a young man about town, tried to learn dancing, and joined elocution classes. But in the end he gave it all up; the cultural barrier of form (not substance) was too high for him to cross. Later, as the secretary of the vegetarian society, he was reinforced in his conviction that the substance—made up of the basic human values found among all people—was the same.

He realized that mastering and remaking himself was far more important than mere appearances. So he stuck to the vow he made to his mother to stay vegetarian. He gave up all food that

151

contained eggs because his mother regarded eggs as meat. Adhering to his word gave him much inner joy and strengthened his willpower. He learned that the "real seat of taste was not the tongue but the mind."[45] And Gandhi commenced his lifelong struggle to control the mind.

Perhaps the greatest gift he got in London was that, for the first time in his life, he read *Bhagavad Gita* in Sir Edwin Arnold's translation. The book contains a distillate of Indian spiritual heritage stretching back at least to 6,000 years, as contained in the Vedas and Upanishads. The *Gita* explains the purpose of human life and ways to achieve it. Selflessness in action is a major *Gita* teaching that Gandhi took to heart. Many years later he wrote about this textbook on living by human values in order to reach the goal of life, describing it thus: "When doubts haunt me, when disappointments stare me in the face and I see not one ray of light on the horizon, I turn to *Gita*, and find a verse to comfort me; and, I immediately begin to smile in the midst of overwhelming sorrow."[46] He also read the New Testament and the "Sermon on the Mount which went straight to my heart."[47]

Thus equipped with the loftiest values person can acquire to guide him or her in the struggles of life, Gandhi returned to India as a qualified lawyer. He set up practice in Rajkot but was not much of a success. Fortunately he was hired by a Gujarati trader named Dada Abdullah Sheth to go to the British colony of South Africa and argue a lawsuit. It was in that country that Gandhi's real transformation took place. Although he was not even 24 years old, he had already acquired all the virtues he needed to remake himself—truth, willpower, integrity and faith.

The lawsuit required Gandhi to travel from Durban to Pretoria. His client purchased a first-class ticket for him for the overnight train journey. On the way a white man entered the compartment where Gandhi was sitting. Seeing Gandhi, he went away and returned with a railway official, who asked Gandhi to transfer to a third-class compartment. It did not matter that he had a first-class ticket. He was brown, not white. Gandhi refused. So they fetched a policeman, who forced him out of the compartment. He declined to travel in a third-class compartment and sat the whole night shivering in the waiting room. His overcoat was in his luggage in the custody of the policeman, and Gandhi refused to go and ask him for it. The next morning he traveled by coach to Johannesburg so that he could finish the remaining portion of his journey to Pretoria.

That night in the waiting room of the railway station triggered all that was noble in Gandhi into resisting injustice. He did not pay heed to the advice a rich Indian merchant gave to him at Johannesburg. He told Gandhi, "This country is not for men like you. For making money we do not mind pocketing insults and here we are [alluding to his wealth]."[48] Gandhi examined the legal position, and when he was certain that Indians were not barred from traveling in first class, he insisted on it and traveled the remaining journey in that class. He galvanized the Indian community to demand equality as citizens. The battle begun that night lasted for 20 years. But it was a battle without hatred. Gandhi evolved and used the technique of passive resistance.

One event in these 20 years indicates Gandhi's broad vision supported by action and is worth mentioning in this very brief story of the formative years of his eventful life. The Boer War was fought from 1889 to 1902, when the Dutch-speaking Boers revolted against British rule. The sympathy of the Indians in South Africa, most of whom were taken to that country as laborers to work on farms, was with the Boer. The Indians had done well for themselves in Africa, many leaving the farms and entering other walks of life. But they did not like the British, who discriminated against them. Gandhi advised them that as citizens of a British colony, it was their moral duty to support the British, irrespective of the injustice done to them. He raised and himself headed an Indian ambulance corps of 1,100 African-born Hindus, Christians and Muslims. They were in the thick of the battle many a time, attending to and evacuating wounded soldiers. The British editor of *Pretoria Times*, wrote about their performance during his visit to the battlefront. "I came across Gandhi in the early morning sitting by the roadside eating a regulation army biscuit. Every man in Buller's [the British General's] force was dull and depressed, and damnation was invoked on everything. But Gandhi was stoical in his bearing, cheerful and confident in his conversation, and had a kindly eye. I saw the man and his small undisciplined Corps on many battlefields during the Natal campaign. When service was to be rendered, they were there. Their unassuming dauntlessness cost them many lives."[49]

After his initial outing in South Africa, Gandhi came back to India for a while and set up his practice in Bombay. He was an instant success. However, on fervent request from the South African community, he abandoned his practice worth U.S.$25,000 (equivalent to about U.S.$1 million today) a year"[50] and went to Africa to lead the struggle by his fellow countrymen. The account of his life there is full of trials, jail terms and setbacks and should be read with care. Victory finally came in 1914 when the Smuts-Gandhi Agreement was signed, giving Indians, to a very large extent, a status of some dignity and honor. Gandhi conducted his nonviolent struggle with the full application of human values. He explained that "It was not part of the tactics of Satyagraha to destroy, hurt, humble or embitter the adversary or to win a victory by weakening him ... but by civil resistance, hope, sincerity, chivalry and self-suffering to convince the opponent's brain and conquer his heart."[51] This is obvious from extracts of a letter written to Gandhi by Field Marshal Jan Smuts, then Prime Minister of South Africa. He said, "You helped us in the days of our need. How can we lay hands on you?... You refuse to injure the enemy.... You desire victory by self-suffering, and never transgress your self-imposed limits of courtesy and chivalry. And, that is what reduces us to sheer helplessness."[52] Smuts and Gandhi became lifelong friends.

154

Gandhi returned to India in 1915, and for the next 32 years led the Indians in their struggle for independence till it was won in 1947. This nonviolent struggle was spearheaded by Gandhi with the firm belief that every man is essentially divine: Consequently, truth and justice would always prevail. However, this can happen only if you morally convince your adversary that your struggle does not mean hurting or humiliating him. His faith in the innate decency of the British character was so strong that he did not consider upper-class Tories who were dead-set against Indian independence as enemies of India. He felt they were prisoners of the prejudice of "us" versus "them" within their own class-ridden society, as well as of their patronizing approach to the colonies. Gandhi's attempt was to convert them to the concept of "us" only—the concept in India's heritage, of looking at humanity, nay, the whole universe, as *one*.

He was also fully convinced that the British were ruling India because of severe weaknesses that had developed in Indian society. In 1909, while in South Africa, he had written a booklet *Indian Home Rule*. He waged his struggle according to the blueprint in that book. Hindu-Muslim unity, removal of untouchability and promotion of homespun cloth as a symbol for uplifting Indian villages were as important as the political struggle for independence.

He discarded his European clothes and dressed like an Indian villager. Living a simple spartan, life, he waged the struggle for India's independence without any dogmas. "He was so open to conviction and had such extraordinary amount of moral courage that, once he was convinced that any particular action of which he was the author was defective, he never hesitated to correct himself and declare publicly that he was wrong."[53] He had that rare combination of leadership and tenacity in reaching the goal, but also the flexibility of mind to alter the method of achieving it. Studying the details of his participation in the struggle for independence amply shows this capability—however, with one very major qualification:

> He never allowed himself to use wrong means to attain the right ends. His punctiliousness in the choice of means was so great, that even the achievement of the end was subordinated to the nature of means used, because he believed that right end could not be achieved by wrong means.[54]

Gandhi's struggle to win independence for India climaxed during World War II. Two great men were pitched in this final battle—Gandhi and British prime minister Winston Churchill, who also is a subject of study in this chapter. "Churchill and Gandhi were alike, in that each gave his life to a single cause."[55] Churchill's one passion in life was to maintain Britain as the primary power in the world. What was the British Empire without its crown jewel—India. Consequently, any talk of India's independence was an anathema to him. India was his blind spot. He was utterly convinced that a democratic world led by British aristocracy would bring peace, opportunity and plenty for all. Gandhi, on the other hand, was totally committed to India's independence. But his vision was loftier. He saw the human race as one large family. He was against fascism and wanted a free India fighting on the side of the democracies. He declared, "I do not want England to be defeated or humiliated. ... I can keep India intact and its freedom intact only if I have goodwill towards the whole human family, and not merely for the human family which inhabits this little spot on the earth called India."[56] And it is here that we see a link between Gandhi, Churchill and Franklin, another statesman with a lofty vision,—the first person studied in this chapter.

About 150 years earlier than Gandhi, Franklin was unable to persuade the British Ministers to grant home rule to the colonies in America. That led to the American War of Independence and the emergence of the USA. During World War II Churchill could not see the great wisdom in Gandhi's advice. Unfortunately, power makes people myopic, and Churchill tenaciously resisted the advice of a number of his own colleagues, as well as that of American president Franklin D. Roosevelt. He insisted on the unconditional surrender of Germany and no independence for India. Churchill won the war but lost the British Empire. Great Britain emerged from the harrowing experience of war, tired and virtually bankrupt. In the first elections after the war, the Tories led by Churchill, the symbol of British aristocracy, were swept out of power. The Labor Party came to rule England, which then granted independence to India.

But it was a victory Gandhi did not relish. The country was partitioned into India and Pakistan. Gandhi was aware that dividing the country on communal lines would hurt everyone, but it would hurt the Muslims most. Unfortunately, the game of divide and rule played by some of the Tories in England blinded the Muslim leadership in India to this cardinal fact. It is of interest to note that dividing India on communal lines was first proposed in 1923 in a book by a staunch Hindu leader, Bhai Parmanand, and in 1924 in a series of articles written by Lala Lajpat Rai and published in the *Tribune*.[57] To Gandhi, who looked at humanity as one, it was a painful experience to find out how the concept of Pakistan became an obsession with Jinnah, its founder. The communal riots that developed after the division pained Gandhi no end. So he took up his old task—"to assuage, to spread love and to make all men brothers."[58]

Throughout his life Gandhi resisted the temptation of power, and his goal was *to be* and not *to have*. Gandhi enriched politics with ethics. He clearly saw the goal of humankind as unity. "Perhaps he will not succeed," wrote India's Nobel Prize-winning poet laureate, Rabindranath Tagore, of the living Gandhi. "Perhaps he will fail as the Buddha failed and as Christ failed to wean men from their inequities, but he will always be remembered as one who made his life a lesson for all ages to come."[59] He will be remembered most when the human race reaches its goal of unity, which is not too far away.

Every young person who wishes to find a true purpose in life and live with joy, peace and laughter should study Gandhi's life. For a start, it would be appropriate to read *The Life of Mahatma Gandhi* by Louis Fischer. The next reading should be his autobiography, *The Story of My Experiments with Truth*. No human being has ever written about himself with such honesty and transparency as Gandhi. And finally, if inspired, study the 18 volumes of the *Collected Works of Mahatma Gandhi*. No one "who takes a dip into Gandhiji's stream of life as represented in this series will emerge disappointed, for there lies in it buried a hidden treasure out of which everyone can carry as much as he likes according to his own capacity and faith."[60]

Sir Winston Churchill

Sir Winston Churchill stands among the tallest of leaders in the twentieth century. His finest hour was when, during World War II (1938-45), he, as the Prime Minister of Great Britain, rallied the world against the tyranny of fascism and scored an unqualified victory. Among his numerous achievements as a soldier, author and statesman, his greatest was Sir Winston himself! The story of how the "troublesome young boy," who stayed at the very bottom of his class throughout his school years transformed himself will inspire every young boy or girl in any age.

His life reveals a sterling character and the truth that "magnanimity, love of reading and a bubbling sense of humor are not incompatible with determination, courage and high seriousness [vision]."[61] Winston was born on November 30, 1874, in a leading aristocratic political family in England. Two qualities ran as a thread through his character during his life—supreme self-confidence and tenacious determination.

158

As a boy, he did not take kindly to his studies. At the age of five, when he "was to be first menaced by education"[62] at the hands of his governess, Winston hid himself in the shrubberies in the woods near his vast home. Many hours passed before he was retrieved! He was immensely distressed when a few months later he had to "descend into a dismal bog called sums ... just as I managed to tackle a particular class of affliction, some other much more variegated type was thrust upon me."[63]

At the age of seven, he was sent to a preparatory boarding school. Winston detested it. He read books beyond his age, but routine studies, particularly in Latin and Greek, bored him to arrogant indifference. He became seriously ill and had to be slowly nursed back to health. After his recovery, he was sent to another preparatory school, which he liked better.

At the age of 12, he was sent to Harrow, the classy English boarding school. He gamely maintained his position at the bottom of the class throughout his stay! His father once enquired of him if he would like to join the army. Thinking that the old man had spotted a special military genius in him, he promptly said yes. Only after many years did he find out that his father had made the suggestion because he thought Winston was not "clever enough to go to the Bar!"[64]

At school, he excelled only in fencing, poetry and writing English. He found the rest of his studies boring. However, he greatly enjoyed listening to the occasional guest speakers, who spoke on a variety of real-life happenings and concerns. Once a guest lecturer spoke on the "Imperial Federation," meaning the developing British Commonwealth. The speaker referred to the famous message Lord Nelson sent on the eve of the sea battle at Trafalgar. The message—"England expects that every man will do his duty"—ran down the battle line. The speaker went on to visualize that "if we and our colonies are held together a day would come when such a signal would run not merely along a line of ships, but along a line of nations."[65] These words gave Churchill a vision of the great role Britain could play in the world. That vision stayed with him throughout his life.

While at Harrow, he twice failed the examination to qualify for entrance to the military academy for officer training. Consequently, he left Harrow and joined a "teaching shop," which prepared boys for this examination. He barely scraped through in his third attempt!

In March 1885, a little before he was 21 years old, Churchill was appointed an officer in a cavalry regiment, the Fourth Hussars. At about the same time his father passed away. He was always very fond of his mother, but this tragedy brought them even closer. Using all her contacts in high political circles, she did her best to help her willful son during his youth.

A year after his father died, Winston moved with his regiment to Bangalore, India. This event triggered in him an immense thirst for learning. Questions like What are Ethics? Who was Aristotle? Why did the government put him to death? started bothering him consistently. About a hundred years ago, Bangalore did not have the enormous educational facilities or the well-stocked libraries of today. So he wrote to his mother, who dutifully, and with great dispatch, started sending him the books he asked for.

Almost every day, during the next couple of years, he read four to five hours a day. He devoured great classics like the eight volumes of *The History of the Decline and Fall of the Roman Empire* by Edward Gibbon, Plato's *Republic, Politics of Aristotle* by Weldon, *Studies in Pessimism* by Arthur Schopenhauer, *An Essay on Principle of Population* by Thomas Malthus and *The Origin of Species* by Charles Darwin. In the absence of a teacher, he developed himself by reflection, analysis and inquiry, while reading these and other great works. He memorized many of Bartlett's *Familiar Quotations* because they "give you good

160

thoughts. They also make you anxious to read the author and look for more."[66]

All this reading inevitably made him reflect on religion and faith. He dismissed as silly the arguments of reason and logic given by science that "nothing is true except what we comprehend."[67] His faith in the Supreme Creator was unflinching. As the years rolled by, his faith became stronger, as happens with all soldiers who come under enemy fire and survive! He prayed to the Creator throughout his life and invariably "I got what I wanted." [68] He learned that true faith was "when you tried your best to live an honorable life, and did your duty, and were faithful to your friends and not unkind to the weak and poor."[69] His faith was the source of his self-confidence.

Instinct told him that he should enrich his reading by actual experience. He knew that in the field of his chosen profession, the military, actual combat is a great educator—not merely for the art of war but for understanding the true nature of people and appropriately dealing with them. So, with the help of his mother's contacts, he was able to participate in active operations in Cuba; against the Pathan tribals in Malakand, India; and at the final battle for Khartoum, in the Sudan. During these sallies, while on leave from his regiment, he wrote for newspapers and was lauded as a competent war correspondent.

His success with the pen induced him to convert his battle experience into two books *The Story of the Malakand Field Force* and *The River War,* which was about the Sudan War. He spent long hours writing and rewriting the chapters of his books. "For three to four hours in the middle of every day, often devoted to slumber or cards saw me industrially at work."[70]

His first book was an instant success. He was praised for its contents as well as for the style of his writing. Comments like "wisdom and comprehension far beyond his years" gave him great

161

joy, especially when contrasted with those he was used to at school—"indifferent," "untidy," "slovenly," "bad" and "very bad"! The book brought him to the attention of the prime minister, who invited him for a chat on the conditions prevailing in northwest India.

He played polo every day and loved it. And, in many ways, it made a major contribution in developing his potential as a leader. "Polo, "he wrote," is the prince of games because it combines all the pleasures of hitting a ball, which is the foundation of so many amusements, with all the pleasures of riding and horsemanship, and to both of these there is added that intricate, loyal teamwork which is the essence of football or base ball and which renders a true combination so vastly superior to individuals of which it is composed."[71]

After about four years of service, he decided to leave the army. The pay was not enough to support the lifestyle of a cavalry officer. And he did not want to be a burden on his widowed mother. He realized that he could earn much more by writing for books and newspaper articles.

He returned home and was promptly picked by the Conservative Party to run in a by-election for Parliament, which he lost. At about this time war clouds were gathering in South Africa. A newspaper offered him a well-paid job covering the war. He accepted the job with alacrity and sailed for South Africa with dispatch.

Trying to be in the thick of battle, he was taken as a prisoner by the Boers. Within a month, he had escaped from prison and was trying to work his way to safety. During this exciting adventure, after two nights of movement in the heart of enemy territory, he was hungry, exhausted and totally dispirited. At this crucial moment, he prayed ardently to the Creator for help and guidance. He started to move again on foot. As if in a stupor, he staggered

162

towards a dimly-lit house in the middle of a vast plain. He desperately needed food and rest. What if the big house was that of a Boer? He would be promptly sent back to prison. Again, subconsciously, he brushed aside these thoughts and knocked on the door. Soon he found himself with the owner—a British settler in South Africa who was working at a coal mine! Providence had guided him well. Churchill was hidden in a coal mine till he was smuggled out to safety in a goods train by his countryman. His escape story made him a bit of a hero.

After the situation in South Africa stabilized somewhat and the British recovered from their reverses of the first two years or so, Churchill returned home. In the elections held soon after, he was elected to Parliament, a success that launched his long and distinguished career in politics. He held responsible ministerial positions during World War I and became the Prime Minister during World War II.

The vision of Great Britain as the pivot of a unified world, which Churchill developed as a schoolboy, lived with him throughout his political life; to him, political power was poetry. It was this vision that made him a vocal and resolute opponent of any attempts to grant independence to India, the largest colony— indeed, the crown jewel of the British empire. It was this view that pitched him against Mahatma Gandhi, who was the father of the movement for India's independence. In November 1942, when Churchill was the prime minister of the British national government waging World War II, he blocked all suggestions even promising independence to India after the war. He summed up his attitude in a well-known quip he made then, "I have not become the King's First Minister in order to preside over the liquidation of British Empire." Like his predecessors, who had refused to grant self-government to the American colonies and thus had missed an opportunity for a permanent linkage between the two states, Churchill maintained a policy that led to missing such a linkage between Great Britain and India. Churchill, a product of the conservative Victorian Era, was unable to rise higher than the vision of a unified world benevolently ruled by British aristocracy, under the thin veil of English-speaking people.

Peace, opportunity and plenty for all was his vision for the world, but a world led by the British aristocracy. This bias was not acceptable even to the British people, and his party was voted out of power soon after World War II. An ardent exponent of English language, he hoped that one day it might play some small part in "the unity of the whole world."[72] This indeed is already happening. He laid the foundation for his outstanding leadership by dint of his tenacious willpower, working long hours while his peers slept or wasted their time otherwise. His advice to the young is loud and clear:

> "You have not an hour to lose. You must take your place in life's fighting line. Twenty to twenty-five! These are the years! Don't be content with things as they are. The earth is yours in fullness thereof. Enter upon your inheritance, accept your responsibility—Don't take "NO" for an answer. Never submit to failure. Do not be fobbed off with mere personal success or acceptance. You will make all kinds of mistakes; but, as long as you are generous and true, and also fierce you cannot hurt the world or even seriously distress it. She was made to be wooed and won by youth."[73]

Winston Churchill's life will inspire to great effort anyone who aspires to an ideal higher than himself or herself. For a start, read about his life in *My Early life*; *A Roving Commission*. Among his other works the two that must be read are the volumes of *A History of the English-Speaking Peoples* and *The Second World War*. If you read them before you turn 20, vast horizons will open up for you.

164

Note for Teachers

Keeping young adults motivated enough to persist in efforts at transforming their character is a most challenging task for the teacher. Nothing succeeds like success. Consequently, the secret of success in this onerous duty lies in choosing the first goal with great care. As we discussed in chapter 7, an aspirant should be guided to choose his or her first target for transformation very deliberately. The goal should not be too difficult to achieve. One victory normally triggers off a momentum that gathers strength as time passes.

Reading about the lives of Benjamin Franklin, Mahatma Gandhi and Winston Churchill does wonders for most young adults. However, a paucity of good books about them and other great lives can pose difficulties. So it is useful to have multiple copies of popular biographies. *The Encyclopaedia Britannica* (and others) give useful leads for detailed studies on most of the lives listed at the end of this book.

Informal tutorial discussion of biographies by a small group of students in the teacher's home always proves very effective. This technique should be used, if possible.

9

The Role of Parents and Teachers in Grooming Leaders

Parents and teachers have always played a decisive role in up-gradating the quality of people in different parts of the world. Civilizations reach their golden age, their pinnacle, when parents are aware of their fundamental duty to groom their children as ideal men and women and when teachers exist who are worthy of this noble profession. This happens when both parents and teachers are conscious that the "ideal of education, all training, should be this man-making."[1] Unfortunately, however, for a long time, and certainly in the current century of "industrial economics," we have tended to get carried away by the outer tinsel of education rather than building a solid core. What use is the tinsel outside when there is no solid inside? The ultimate aim of all training is to make people grow. "The man who influences, who throws his magic, as it were, on his fellow beings, is a dynamo of power."[2] When societies have leaders of such mettle whose *to be* is strong and well balanced, then families, institutions, communities and nations start acquiring a touch of enduring excellence. For grooming such men and women, parents and teachers must ensure that children "grow up in an atmosphere of reverence, devotion, mutual service and ... cooperation."

Now they learn only copybook maxims, devoid of any sincere urge to put them into practice. Parents drink, gamble, scandalize others and utter blatant lies in the full hearing of these tender flowers. Do not sow hatred or contempt for any caste or class, faith or cult, in the virgin minds of those fresh blossoms. Parents first, teachers next, playmates and companions later, and elders who command the allegiance of community or region last have to be on the alert, constantly

166

examining themselves to see whether they are fit examples for the children of the land.[3]

In the progressive development of man, it is well to remember his final destination. Maslow (1908-72, the father of humanistic psychology, which emphasizes the study of well-adjusted, rather than maladjusted people in understanding human nature) has presented the growth of man in his "hierarchy of needs," as explained in chapter 6. He was in the final stages of his life when he realized that a man's highest needs are spiritual. And that these needs give enduring happiness when fulfilled. Parents and teachers have to guide their wards on the spiritual path. The secret of success in fulfilling spiritual needs is to "start early, drive slowly and reach safely."[4] The spiritual foundation of children—based on the universal human values of truth, right conduct, love, equanimity and noninjury—should be laid very early in their lives.

First and foremost, children have to be raised to become persons of character. There is no way—absolutely none—by which children can be molded other than by personal example set by parents and teachers. So, in this challenging obligation, the first need for both is to examine themselves to see if they are worthy of emulation. If not, then the only real contribution they can make in rearing children is to transform themselves. For the sake of convenience, the description of a person of character is reproduced below. Such a person is:

An honest man;

a man with a sense of duties and obligations of his position, whatever it may be;

a man who tells the truth;

a man who gives others their due;

a man considerate to the weak;

a man who has principles and stands by them;

167

a man not too elated by good fortune and not too depressed by bad;

a man who is loyal;

a man who can be trusted.[5]

Let there be no reservation in the mind of any parent or teacher about having the ability to transform his or her own character. It is the right of every human being. All that is needed to achieve this goal is a sincere and persistent effort. The reward is massive; perhaps, the most attractive benefit is enduring personal happiness, as explained in chapter 7.

The Role of Parents

"The earth is a common soil in which we grow all types of trees. If we sow neem seed (a tree with bitter leaves and seeds), naturally a neem tree will grow. If we sow a mango, we will get a mango tree. A mother is like earth. To beget children, the conduct of the parents acts like the seed that is sown."[6] This assertion sums up the role of parents in grooming leaders.

The mother is the main architect of the character of her children. That is why a mother is such a hallowed person all over the world. In India a mother is classed with God, "God could not be everywhere, so he made mothers."[7] It is a fact of history that the character of every outstanding leader was formed by the influence of his mother.

We have seen in chapter 8 the tremendous influence mothers had on the character and progress of Mahatma Gandhi and Winston Churchill in their very formative years.

The role of a mother, not only in rearing children but in building nations, is lucidly described in these words:

Motherhood is the most precious gift of God. Mothers are the makers of a nation's fortune or misfortune, of the shape and the sinews of the soul. These sinews are toughened by lessons they should teach: fear of sin and fondness of virtue. Both are based on faith in God being the inner motivator of all. If you want to know how advanced a nation is, study the mothers. Are they free from fear and anxiety? Are they full of love towards all? Are they trained in fortitude and virtue? If you would like to imbibe the glory of a culture, watch its mothers rocking the cradle, and feeding, fostering, teaching and fondling babies. As the mother, so the progress of the nation; as the mother, so the sweetness of the culture.[8]

In the cyclic rise and fall of Indian civilization, which has survived more than 6,000 years, there is an important lesson on the role of the mother. In true Indian culture a mother has always occupied a place even above God. But in the latest millennium the decline in India is related to the fall in status of its women.

Slowly, over a period of a few centuries, Indian womanhood has been displaced from its lofty pedestal of motherhood and reverence. This happens in most prosperous societies when they are obsessed with material wealth and sensuous pleasures and start rolling in luxury. A woman then becomes an object of sensuality, rather than reverence.

Fortunately for the country, the tradition of reverence for motherhood survived in rural India, and that will enable this ancient land, once again, to rise to an era of glory and well-being. This is illustrated by the example of a rural mother who groomed her son to become a star of The Indian Renaissance. However, before we look at this example, let us, for a moment, ponder over the words of Arnold Toynbee, the famous historian, on motherhood in the history of the world: "The mother in the home environment

169

is irreplaceable as the educator of her children in the early years of life during which a child's character and temperament are formed. Part of a child's personality is determined by the genes. But, the character is formed by an interaction between a person's heredity and his response to his environments, and it seems to be agreed that, though character can be modified at all stages of life, the decisive developments occur during the first five years, and that, at this formative age, the major environmental agency is the mother's educational influence."[9] Those who miss loving motherhood retain deep scars in their character for life. And now, let's look at the example of a rural mother in India.

In a village named Birsingha, near Calcutta, lived a Brahmin family in great poverty. It was a large joint family. The eldest son, who had little formal education, had to move to Calcutta when he was barely 15 years old to earn money and send it to his family in the village. When he was 18, he got married and later had a son. For the first eight years of his life, this young boy was brought up by his mother in the village.

The young mother, a lady of wisdom and virtue, started to groom her son with love, tender care and discipline. At the age of five, he was sent to the makeshift private school that was available in the village. His mother took deep interest in his lessons. But she also emphasized that he should not merely study for worldly knowledge, but acquire spiritual insight into life itself—that practicing human values was far more important than observing prevailing rituals and dogmas. Worldly education was necessary to earn a living, but he should never become a parasite on society. Above all, she convinced him that sensual pleasures of the world were not important and that only the foolish men enter that path.

With unselfish love, the mother saw to it that at the age of eight he was sent with his father to Calcutta for higher education. She was content to see her son during holidays when father and son

170

would walk to their village. The boy excelled in his studies, grew up, got a job and started working with dedication and honesty.

One day, when at home in the village, he saw his mother getting ready to participate in the village fair. It was the custom then for women to dress up in their best clothes and wear their ornaments to the fair. His mother had no jewelry. So the son offered to buy her some ornaments, but she lovingly declined. She said, "I do want three ornaments, but I will ask you to get these for me sometime later."

A few more years went by. Due to his good character, diligence and efficiency, this young man was promoted. He felt that it was an appropriate occasion to get the three ornaments his mother had spoken about. But when he tried to persuade her to name the three, she again declined, saying, "Not yet." I shall ask you for them a little later."

The time rolled by. The son became head of the institution where he was working. A printing press and a publishing house that he had set up also flourished. He again broached the subject of the three ornaments. This time the mother relented. She said hers was not the age to wear ornaments. The jewelry she wanted was of a different type. Then slowly, she named the three ornaments she wanted from him:

Our village does not have a proper primary school for small children. They have to walk two miles to reach one. Get a small school started in the village.

There are no medical facilities in our village. When women and children fall ill, they have a very difficult time. Set up a small dispensary in the village.

The third ornament I want is your behavior. It should always be worthy of my name. Never be lured by money.

171

What a lofty mother she must have been. Little wonder that her son became Ishwar Chandra Vidyasagar—the giant of the Indian Renaissance during the nineteenth century.

Vidyasagar, meaning "the ocean of learning," was the title conferred on him by his college for his outstanding academic record. Among the tall social leaders and reformers who pioneered the Indian Renaissance, Ishwar Chandra was rightly referred to as the "first among us."[10] He was credited with having "the genius and wisdom of an ancient sage, the energy of an Englishman, and the heart of a Bengali mother."[11] He fought battles for modern education, widow remarriage and antipolygamy. Above all, he practiced human values, silently trying to persuade people to graduate from religion to spirituality; his character spoke more eloquently than the words of preachers.

Modern research is coming to some interesting conclusions on the role of the mother in building the character of individuals. The process starts when the child is still in the womb. What she does, her moods and her food have a profound effect on the child. The most balanced, well-adjusted and warm-hearted individuals are those who have been virtually inseparable from their mothers for the first two years of their childhood. In countries and regions where babies are constantly carried by their mothers during the first six months, even while doing the daily chores of housework, children grow up to be the happiest of adults, even in adversity.

There is also another side to the mother's role in molding the character of her children. Sometime back a scholar carried out a study on the way mothers bring up children, comparing how Israeli and Indian mothers handle a child learning to walk. This study brings out several characteristic differences in the perception of Israelis vis-à-vis Indians, but one is worth noting. An Israeli mother stands at the other end of the room and encourages the toddler to walk towards her. If on the way the child topples, she does not rush to pick him or her up even though the child is crying. Instead, she encourages the toddler to stand up and walk again on his or her own. When the child finally reaches her, she gives him or her all the love and affection. On the other hand, most Indian mothers handle the same situation differently. They too encourage the child to walk. However, if on the way the child topples, falls and cries, then they rush to pick him or her up. That is not the end of the story. They start beating the floor and say, "Naughty floor has hurt my child." At this, the child stops crying. At the same time, the child also gets a firm conviction in his or her mind that "if any misfortunes were ever to happen, or in the event of failure, he could put the blame on somebody else!"[12]

Young people who have such an attitude firmly ingrained in their personality from childhood are unsuitable material for leading others. Fortunately, there are still numerous mothers in India who do inculcate self-reliance and other good qualities and traits in their children. However, there is a great need to spread this essential awareness among mothers the world over.

While the mother is the child's first guide, the second, before the teacher steps in, is the father. He has to devote time to the family if the harmonious and happy environment needed for the children to grow up to be well-adjusted adults is to prevail. Admittedly, his major contribution is the example he sets through his conduct. It is his duty to see that the 10 cardinal rules[13] of bringing up children are used in the family:

- Treat all your children with equal affection.

- Make their friends welcome in your home.

- Do not quarrel in front of the children.

- Be truthful to each other.

- Never lie to them.

- Always answer their queries.

173

- Do not punish them in the presence of others.

- Be constant in your moods and affections.

- Keep close to them.

- Concentrate on their good points and not their failures.

In industrial societies a large proportion of married couples try to adjust their lives in a way that allows both husband and wife to work. Whatever be the compulsions for such an arrangement, a good deal of experience has been gained about it during the last 60 years or so. It is not easy to generalize, but by and large, the impact on such couples' children, brought up by nannies or relatives or in nursery schools, has been adverse. The growing opinion among those who have been through it all and can look back with some detachment is that the wife should work, if at all, only after the youngest child is five years old.

The Purpose of Education

Before we discuss the role of teachers, it would be useful to take a brief look at the purpose of education and the educational system that has proven again and again to be an effective nursery for producing leaders. The enduring purpose of education is contained in the ancient Indian scripture, the *Taittariya Upanishad*. A crisp Sanskrit sloka reads:

Satyam Vada, Dharmam Chara

The word *dharma* is not easy to translate, and has innumerable connotations. It is a whole concept and not merely a word. The nearest translation into English would be:

> Speak the truth and act as an ideal man who has a sense of duties and obligations of his position, whatever it may be.

174

Thus, the purpose of education focuses on truth, duties and obligations of a person to his family, to society and to humanity at large.

The Sai university has adopted this Upanishadic phrase as its motto. The university is a modern enlarged version of a *gurukula*, literally meaning "the home of the teacher [guru], or a *rishi-kula,* "the home of the saint [rishi]," referring to the individuals who accepted boys[14] to be made rich with:

- the wealth of wisdom

- the gold mine of character

- the treasure of culture

It will be interesting to see how this system works in an industrialized country in the West, to fully appreciate its impact on society.

Great Britain is a small island. During the eighteenth and nineteenth centuries, the British were able to carve out the largest empire ever created in history. It used to be said that "The sun never sets on the British Empire." How did they do it? Analysis shows that the factor that contributed most towards this achievement was the educational system the British adopted. The system was the result of a conscious decision made when they realized their society had seriously degenerated. They undertook to inject moral values through their educational system.

The main component of this effort was the public school system (in fact, the term *public school* originally meant "private residential school.") Unfortunately, this institution has since become a preserve for wards of moneyed people in Great Britain, as well as in India, where it was adopted during the early years of this century. However, when originally conceived, evolved and consolidated, the public school was meant for promising boys from

175

all strata of society. In essence, the system was a westernized version of the *gurukula*. It was built around the *house master*—a teacher in whose house boys lived exactly as in the guru's house in India. House masters, and their wives, became the foster parents of the children, providing a loving home for them to learn good manners and the discipline of harmonious living. The sons of kings and commoners were taken away from parental care to live in the master's house and be groomed on the basis of the following two important principles:

First, the school allowed the children to grow up in an atmosphere of complete social equality. When they reached the house of the master (public schools had, and continue to have, a number of house masters), parental clothes were taken away and all the children had to live and work in their school uniform. They slept in the same type of beds, mixed together without let or hindrance, ate the same food, and had exactly the same facilities in the master's house (as numbers grew, dormitories were built, but these, even now, are designated as houses). Above all, every child was allowed a very frugal and strictly controlled uniform pocket money. In such a common social environment, the children developed their potential without inhibitions or social hang-ups or handicaps related to their parents' standing in society. The house master, like the guru, became the key figure in molding the character of the boys. The position as house master was a highly honored and extremely well-paid appointment given to teachers of proven ability and character.

The second principle was that building the character of the boys was the main function of the school. In every facet of life in the school, (whether related to living, studying, games or extracurricular activities) much more emphasis was placed on team performance than on individual achievement. Universal human values—like truth, honesty, integrity, loyalty, courage and determination—were imparted in day-to-day functioning. Comradeship and sharing were encouraged to inculcate selflessness. Sundays were exclusively devoted to understanding the Supreme Creator and the spiritual basis of life. In short, the boys were groomed to be the future leaders of society and of the nation at large.

The intrinsic value of this system of education was that it "made a boy independent. He left home early and had to look after himself. He learned to believe that there was something praiseworthy about enduring hardship without complaint. He was taught to own a fault and take punishment without bearing a grudge.... He learned that to command, he must be just and impartial and must put the comfort and safety of those under him before his own."[15] All this was possible because in the public school system much of the school life was and continues to be run by the older boys. They are given an opportunity to exercise authority and responsibility. To be a "head boy" of the school is a high honor, but responsibilities like the "house captain" or the "school head boy" are, as Toynbee observes, given to chosen older boys as "a test of character."[16]

The impact of the schooling system that we have just discussed was remarkable. Within 50 years, it started providing effective leaders with lofty ideals to the British Parliament, industry, commerce, armed forces, professions and the educational system itself, which ultimately laid the foundations of the vast British Empire.

If parents and teachers fully appreciate the real purpose of education, then many schools can be transformed in the same way as the ideal schools we have discussed. However, this is possible only if the chosen schools are liberated from the shackles of government bureaucracy. In the entire scheme of things, the quality of teachers plays the most crucial role.

177

The Role of Teachers

A teacher must have the wisdom and sense of humor to be able to laugh instead of being uncomfortable with the well-known quip of George Bernard Shaw: "He who can, does. He who cannot, teaches!"

Teachers should laugh even louder on listening to the extension of the quip: "He who can neither do nor teach becomes a consultant!" And they should laugh the loudest on listening to its final version: "He who can do none of the three, becomes the principal of a college"!

A teacher has good reason to laugh because the quip is essentially related to imparting knowledge. As we have discussed earlier, knowledge, though important, forms merely 10 percent of the capability of an effective leader; the other 90 percent is character. The real role of a teacher, consequently, is "doing" the most challenging work in a society—the work of making men and women and grooming leaders. In a nutshell, a teacher, like an artist, has to shape, enrich and hone the character, wisdom and culture of each individual pupil.

To do this daunting work, a teacher has to be aware of the truth that there is no way—absolutely none—that he or she can succeed without being a person of character, wisdom and culture. "Character is the hallmark of a teacher.... A life without good character is like a shrine without light, a coin that is counterfeit, a kite with the string broken."[17]

An individual's first need as a teacher is to know his or her pupils well. A good teacher:

Knows his pupils better than their mothers do and cares even more. (See chapter 6 on dealing with people.)

To know them so well is no easy task. And caring more than their mothers is even more demanding. A teacher has to be an ocean of love to fulfill this requirement. The exercise on knowing people in chapter 6 is a good starting point for a teacher who wants to know his or her pupils. This first step requires a good deal of time and effort, but without this knowledge we cannot even get started in molding children. It is here that the teacher should set an example of the secret of success in life by demonstrating that "incessant work, self- reliance, fearlessness, cheerfulness, self-denial, universal love and concentration of mind... all true work is rest... when industry and virtue meet and kiss, then the fruit is bliss."[18]

As far as knowledge is concerned, the real role of a teacher, particularly of young adults, is "to teach them to educate themselves."[19] Instead of stuffing the minds of his or her pupils with information, a teacher should encourage them to dive deeply into libraries and learn "by industrious work, deep concentration and inner power to struggle hard against the storm of unfavorable circumstances."[20]

Concentration is a great virtue that a teacher has to teach. Ordinary human beings waste 90 percent of thought force and, consequently, make mistakes. Centuries of experience in developing this crucial ability is embodied in the following words:

Take up one idea. Make that one idea your life; think of it, dream of it, live on that idea; let the brain, the muscles, nerves, every part of your body be full of that idea; and just leave every other idea alone. This is the way to success."[21]

It is by such concentrated steps that teachers can mold the character of their pupils. Once we learn to concentrate on the work in hand, then we really realize that "to err is not human."[22] Mastery of the subject and communication skills enable a teacher to impart the knowledge he or she has to teach in the class. But the teacher's primary role—to build character, to instill wisdom and to steep his or her pupils in culture—needs very much more from a teacher. Most of these goals can be achieved, essentially, through group activities.

The well-known saying that "the Battle of Waterloo was won on the playing fields of Harrow and Eton" has a deep significance. It does not mean that sporting skills of the participating leaders won the battle. It refers to the influence that group games had on the character of this battle's military leaders, who had been educated at public schools named Harrow and Eton and others like them. Group games inculcate "that intricate and loyal teamwork which is the essence of football or base ball, and which renders a true combination so vastly superior to individuals of which it is composed."[23]

Participants in group games played in well-knit teams learn that:

- The team is more important than themselves.

- They have to curb selfishness and cooperate for the team to win.

- No sacrifice is too big if it contributes to the victory of the team.

- Personal likes and dislikes must be kept in check for a bigger cause—the team.

- In order to become a good leader, they must learn to give their best when being led by a team captain.

Tutorial groups are a very useful means for deriving the fullest benefit from reading about great lives and studying other classics. Students can be divided into tutorial groups of not more than nine (odd numbers promote better discussion and activity, with one individual emerging as a leader when it is necessary). They read the prescribed book on their own and then periodically meet in the teacher's home for an informal discussion. The intellectual stimulation that such discussions provide creates a lasting impact on the minds of the individuals. It also provides an opportunity for students to get to know one another better, to learn to respect views different from their own and to draw inspiration from the book being read. Above all, it provides the teacher with an opportunity to get to know his or her pupils more intimately and to steer them towards becoming persons of ideal character.

Extracurricular activities like music (especially group singing), dramatics, social work, gardening and the like, provide opportunities for growth of character and should be encouraged.

Many institutions, aware of their character-building role, use the honor code system. It is a technique that essentially inculcates the three cardinal virtues of character included in the word *honesty*. These are not stealing, not lying and not cheating. Peer pressure is the best way to acquire these virtues and is best administered by the student groups themselves—of course, with severe penalties for violation. And this brings us to the role of teachers in disciplining students.

Discipline is defined as "training that corrects, molds or perfects the mental faculties and moral character, behavior that results from such training." Imposed order and behavior under supervision is not real discipline. Real discipline flows from the heart and is visible in an individual's behavior all the time. Thus, discipline is an indication of strength of character and habit. Students should be guided to judge their own strengths by self-inquiry on issues such as:

- Do I, on my own, observe punctuality, cleanliness and order?

- Do I resist the temptation to jump the line?

- Do I keep my word once I say that I will do something?

181

- Am I humble and polite to all?

- Do I work diligently even when I am not being watched?

Should or should not a teacher punish? The best answer to this question is given by an educator, who, during the modern Indian Renaissance, set up a vast chain of Anglo-Vedic educational institutions. "The relationship between a teacher and student should be like that of the parent and the child. But the teacher should not be slow in reprimanding the pupil when needed. He should be a strict disciplinarian. He should rule over the pupils by love and affection."[24] A good mother does not spare the rod when the occasion demands. The same is true of a good teacher, and there is a very good reason for this. If mistakes are overlooked under the false notion that this is love, then the mistakes multiply and become habits. It is the bounden duty of a teacher (as it is of parents) to check mistakes promptly and chastise the pupil. Of course, the best punishment, the one having a lasting impact, is that which is administered privately. This is so because public humiliation makes youth rebellious and resistant to change for the better. However, when the pupils understand that the purpose of chastisement is for their own good, then they accept it with good cheer. Such a response depends entirely on the respect a teacher commands by the qualities of his or her own character, particularly unselfish love.

Group activities that provide maximum opportunities to develop and consolidate character are those undertaken in conditions of danger, fatigue and stress. These activities are also a good test of achievement in character development. An example will explain this point.

An educational institution had a system that, at the end of a semester, required tutorial groups to trek distances of 50 to 100 miles, depending on the class. The grades of individuals in the group depended very much on the performance of the group. The evaluation of the performance included the following:

- Time taken by the group to cover the distance.

- Finishing the trek together, instead of in dribs and drabs. If an individual dropped out, he was required to repeat the semester, and it was a major minus point for the group; *no* exceptions were made other than for fractured bones. The group was expected to help a member who was weak, ill or hurt.

- State of the group's cohesion and team spirit during the trek, as observed by teachers from time to time on the route.

- State of their alertness and cleanliness on finishing the trek. They were administered an objective test appropriate to their class in the college.

Normally, groups took about three to five days to complete the distance. There was a checkpoint every 10 miles or so. The route was mostly through a forest and low hills. The groups were allowed to elect their own leader and plan for all they had to carry to survive for the duration of the trek. It gave the group an opportunity to experience the leadership process and functions explained in chapter 2 of this book.

Those individuals who have been through this institution look back on these treks as major landmarks in their life.

In every group one or two young adults who were a bit weak needed help. This was provided in a very carefully planned manner. The stronger members carried their food, water and other necessities so that they could walk without any burden.

Great innovations were made in packing and carrying the load needed for the trek. The groups would start preparing and practicing well in advance to harden the soles of their feet against blisters, but blisters would come all the same! They carried ample supplies of elastoplast to cover the blisters after they appeared. Many young men would reach the finish line limping and virtually being carried by their teammates; when the elastoplasts were removed, the soles of their feet often looked like raw chunks of red meat. Many walked in spite of fever, cough and cold due to exposure. Those who lost heart were motivated and encouraged by others not to let down the group. They learned a lot.

When they slept, they took turns watching for wild animals, holding strong torches ready to scare them away. They learned how to organize their lives in the wilderness—burning wood to brew tea or to cook, making sure where the water sources were so they could replenish their supply, picking up edible roots and fruits, caring and sharing, and sleeping in the open on Mother Earth. Since they were not allowed to have any money, they learned to strictly ration and conserve the food they carried; in any case, there were only a few villages on the route, and they were not allowed to enter these. They learned to handle emergencies and render first aid when a member tripped and fell down a hillside, a scorpion bit, someone had a bout of vomiting and so on. They learned that slow and steady wins the race. Finally, all participants look back on these treks as a source of strengthening their *willpower,* which has given them tremendous self-confidence in life.

Teachers can start such treks or similar activities anywhere in the world.

Self-centered individualism and the vanity of the selfish life has undermined the duties and obligations (dharma) of parents and teachers to groom children as ideal men and women. This is noticeable all over the world. This trend can rapidly be overcome if societies restore the honor and dignity of teachers to a level noticeable in civilizations that reached their golden age. Teaching in those times was the most honored vocation. Rather than ring our hands and wait for major reforms to take place, we should heed Toynbee's advice: "Man ought to follow love; even if it leads to self-sacrifice. Love is the spiritual impulse to bring the self back into harmony with the rest of the universe, from which self has been estranged by its innate, but not unconquerable, self-centeredness."[25] This is an individual challenge for each parent and teacher.

Good and effective leadership, particularly its ethical and moral core reflected in selflessness, can be easily instilled in children if parents and teachers set the right example. Habits of conduct and behavior that are formed during the growing years can most certainly be changed. But it is not an easy task. Consequently, when we think of the future of our children and their children in the world of the next century, we, the parents and teachers of today have to sit up. It is no use cursing the darkness that looms all around us. Each one of us bears a great responsibility to remove that darkness.

We must constantly focus on building sterling character in our children. But we shall succeed in doing so only if we can transform ourselves for the better by practicing human values. As the adage goes, "An ounce of practice is better than tons of advice."

Epilogue

During the last 150 years or so, the human race has made amazing progress in mastering science and technology. However, like our primitive ancestors we are not the master of the situation in which we find ourselves. The reason is simple. We have failed to master ourselves. The rising wave of violence throughout the world is due to the complete erosion of human values from our conduct. Greed for money and sensual pleasures has become the goal of life.

A very high proportion of children in educational institutions are involved in smoking, drugs, sex, stealing, lying and cheating. Surveys indicate that before they are sixteen, children see on television thousands of acts of violence and by eighteen equally large numbers of scenes that excite sensuality.

Selfless love, which is the foundation of a happy and harmonious life in a family, community and society, is fast disappearing from human behavior. Self-centered individualism with a "me-first" syndrome dominates our lives and is playing havoc with human nature. Divorce rates of about 50 percent in most of the advanced countries are a symptom of this malaise. The result is that proper and loving parenting, which is the main source of character building for future generations, is drying up. As discussed in this book, there can be no effective leadership without character.

On the face of it, the future picture of humanity seems bleak. Yet, this book has been written to groom leaders who would move human race to a new age—the age of Unity of Man, Global Economy and Earth Citizenship. Is there cause for this lofty hope?

The hope lies essentially in our youth. If they seem to be drifting towards self-destructive ways, it is squarely the fault of parents, broken homes, fractured relationships and indifferent upbringing. Just as an atom is the building block of the universe, a family is the building block of human society. In an atom, the protons, neutrons and electrons are held together by the "strong atomic force." A family is held together by the strongest force of all—selfless love. If this central force is removed, then the human race is doomed. Even among the worst victims of the prevailing and rapidly deteriorating deficiencies in moral values, there are many young persons who show palpable hunger to know the "better purpose" of life. Round the world millions of youth who have potential for leadership have the vision of building a better world, a more caring and sharing world—indeed, a more compassionate world. They are looking for a holistic and practical model to fashion their lives on. This book attempts to provide such a model to youth who dare to rise higher than mere selfish greed symbolized by money and sensual pleasures—youth who have courage, willpower and initiative to be the leaders of tomorrow. It is young adults of this category who are hungry to listen to words like the following:

- You can buy a bed, but not sleep.

- You can buy a book, but not brains.

- You can buy food, but not hunger.

- You can buy clothes, but not beauty.

- You can buy medicine, but not health.

- You can buy a house, but not home.

- You can buy luxuries, but not happiness.

- You can buy a crucifix, but not heaven.

- You can buy a temple, but not God.

187

How can we get what money cannot buy? We can get it with our character and with sacrifice. The problem is how to communicate this great truth to youth? How to inspire them to choose the path of future happiness in place of immediate pleasure? This book contains some time-tested truths to be applied in achieving this goal. One factor that, invariably, has won the hearts and minds of people in the most difficult situations is selfless love.

The renowned historian Arnold Toynbee, during the last few years of his long (86-year) life, reflected deeply on the panorama of human progress. During his life he had researched history like no one before him. With clinical detachment, he had looked at the integrated megatrends in the evolution of the human race. He saw how attempts to impose unity on the world by conquest, or through organized religion, had failed. Reflecting on the meaning, purpose and destiny of human life, he was worried about the contemporary situation. He feared that three major developments might lead humans to destroy themselves. In nuclear weapons, the human race had acquired the capability of obliterating all life on the planet many times over. Ever-rising environmental pollution, caused by indiscriminate industrialization, would make the world uninhabitable. To top it all, people had completely lost their moral moorings. He concluded that the only hope for human survival was if "there is unification of mankind." And he opined that such a unification could be brought about only if people become spiritual as the result of a "worldwide spread of some common religion." Can such a miracle take place?

For the last 54 years, Sathya Sai Baba, a man from a small village in India, has been working with single-minded tenacity to bring about this miracle. Operating on different planes and levels, quietly, without fanfare, he is moving humanity towards the blueprint for a global state that he has articulated for the new age. Millions of people round the world are being inspired to change themselves and believe in Sai Baba's spiritual call for unity:

188

"There is only one nation, the nation of humanity;
There is only one language, the language of heart;
There is only one religion, the religion of love;
There is only one God, and he is omnipresent."

The common religion Toynbee talked about is going to be love.

Love, in fact, is the pedestal on which all faiths in the world stand. Unfortunately, this pedestal has gotten buried under human ego, greed and lust for power. It has merely to be rediscovered. There is absolutely no need for a new religion. All religions lead us to the same light, as symbolized in Sai Baba's insignia below:

The man who has been portrayed as the *Embodiment of Love** has described the power of love in very categoric terms. Love that can elevate a human being to his or her reality is "love that needs no requital, love that knows no bargaining, love that is paid gladly as tribute to all living, love that is unwavering; love alone can overcome obstacles, however many and mighty."

The key to effective leadership lies in love. The practical manifestation of love is in removing sorrow from others and in giving happiness to others. That is why the great formula for effective leadership, which enables a leader to demand the

---

*The title of a book on Sai Baba by Peggy Mason and Ron Laing.

impossible for a cause and get it, is based on the example of selfless love of a mother for her infants. Indeed, a leader has to surpass even a mother:

A good leader knows his people better than their
mothers do and cares even more.

The formula works with unfailing success at all levels of leadership—family, institution, community, nation and humanity. To lead, and to lead well, is the most challenging, exciting and joyous role a person can play. It is verily within the reach of everyone who dares to soar higher than mere selfishness.

Bhagavan Sri Sathya Sai Baba

AFTERWORD

LOVE AND LEADERSHIP

The honour of a community is based on its morals;
Without morality a community perishes;
Only a moral community is worth its name;
Bear this in mind : Oh valiant son of Bharat.

The personality of an individual blossoms when he is wedded to morality. Only he can be called a real person who manifests the divinity within him. A man does not become human merely by having the human form. Form is not important. Only conduct counts. Conduct is supremely important.

It is not easy for one and all to manifest their inherent divinity. Only those who have practised self-discipline and lead a good life have the competence to manifest their true personality. Persons who have observed strict discipline and developed the power of discrimination to judge what is right and what is wrong can become ideal leaders by the example of their lives. They must possess individual character and social morality. For achieving this, they have to strive for purity in thought, word and deed.

Love (Prema) is another name for Right Conduct (Dharma). It is also called "priyam", that which is pleasing. The value of love is beyond praise. Love is totally free from selfishness. It knows no distinction of "mine" and "others". Only one who is filled with this love can love society, the nation and the world. His love extends to the whole of society beyond himself and his family. He has to keep in view the well-being of society, the nation and the world. These are the insignia of a true leader.

Those who set up industries and accumulate wealth should not rest content with this. They must have the spirit of sacrifice. People who give advice to others, but do not practise what they preach are hypocrites. It is a travesty of language to call such persons as leaders. Give up selfishness. Have the nation's well-being in view. Develop character and morality. When one sets the example of man who adheres to morals and who loves God and fears sin, he will be able to elevate the morals of the society.

December 1993

With Love

Baba

108 LIVES OF PEOPLE
WHO INSPIRE

1.	Rama	Earlier than 4000 B.C.	India
2.	Bharat	Earlier than 4000 B.C.	India
3.	Valmiki	Earlier than 4000 B.C.	India
4.	Krishna	Earlier than 3000 B.C.	India
5.	Vyasa	Earlier than 3000 B.C.	India
6.	Abraham	Earlier than 2000 B.C.	Turkey & Israel
7.	Moses	During 13th century B.C.	Egypt & Israel
8.	King David	1070-962 B.C.	Israel
9.	Homer	During 8th century B.C.	Greece
10.	Zoroaster	628-551 B.C.	Iran
11.	Cyrus the Great	590-529 B.C.	Iran
12.	Mahavira	599-527 B.C.	India
13.	Buddha	563-483 B.C.	Nepal
14.	Confucius	551-479 B.C.	China
15.	Socrates	469-399 B.C.	Greece
16.	Plato	427-347 B.C.	Greece
17.	Alexander the Great	356-323 B.C.	Greece
18.	Aristotle	384-322 B.C.	Greece
19.	Lao-tzu	During 4th century B.C.	China
20.	Euclid	During 4th century B.C.	Greece & Egypt
21.	Chanakya	During 4th century B.C.	India
22.	Ashoka the Great	300-232 B.C.	India
23.	Shih Huang Ti	259-210 B.C.	China
24.	Patañjali	During 2nd century B.C.	India
25.	Hannibal	247-183 B.C.	Tunisia
26.	Julius Caesar	100-44 B.C.	Italy
27.	Caesar Augustus	63 B.C.-14 A.D.	Italy
28.	Jesus Christ	6 B.C.-30 A.D.	Israel
29.	St. Paul	4-64 A.D.	Turkey
30.	Kalidasa	During 4th century A.D.	India
31.	Vikramaditya	During 4th century A.D.	India
32.	Aryabhata	476-550 A.D.	India

33.	Muhammad	570-632	Saudi Arabia
34.	Adi Shankara	700-738	India
		(sometime as 600)	
35.	Charlemagne	742-814	France
36.	Alfred the Great	849-900	Great Britain
37.	Dante	1265-1321	Italy
38.	Marco Polo	1254-1324	Italy
39.	Joan of Arc	1412-1431	France
40.	Queen Isabella	1451-1504	Spain
41.	Columbus	1451-1506	Italy & Spain
42.	Kabir	1440-1518	India
43.	Leonardo da Vinci	1452-1519	Italy
44.	Desiderius Erasmus	1466-1536	Netherlands& Switzerland
45.	Nanak	1469-1539	India
46.	Martin Luther	1483-1546	Germany
47.	Michelangelo	1475-1564	Italy
48.	Queen Elizabeth	1533-1603	Great Britain
49.	Akbar the Great	1542-1605	India
50.	Shakespeare	1564-1616	Great Britain
51.	Francis Bacon	1561-1626	Great Britain
52.	Galileo Galilei	1564-1642	Italy
53.	Richelieu	1585-1642	France
54.	Oliver Cromwell	1599-1658	Great Britain
55.	Shivaji	1627-1680	India
56.	Peter the Great	1672-1725	Russia
57.	Isaac Newton	1643-1727	Great Britain
58.	Bach	1685-1750	Germany
59.	Rousseau	1712-1778	Switzerland & France
60.	Samuel Johnson	1709-1784	Great Britain
61.	Frederick the Great	1712-1786	Germany
62.	Benjamin Franklin	1706-1790	USA
63.	Adam Smith	1723-1790	Great Britain
64.	George Washington	1732-1799	USA
65.	Kant	1724-1804	Germany
66.	Nelson	1758-1805	Great Britain
67.	James Watt	1736-1819	Great Britain
68.	Napoleon	1769-1821	France

69.	Thomas Jefferson	1743-1826	USA
70.	Beethoven	1770-1827	Germany & Austria
71.	Simon Bolivar	1783-1830	Venezuela
72.	Abraham Lincoln	1809-1865	USA
73.	Charles Darwin	1809-1882	Great Britain
74.	Karl Marx	1818-1883	Germany & Great Britain
75.	Louis Pasteur	1822-1895	France
76.	Bismarck	1815-1898	Germany
77.	Vivekananda	1863-1902	India
78.	Jamshetji Tata	1839-1904	India
79.	Florence Nightingale	1820-1910	Great Britain
80.	Leo Tolstoy	1828-1910	Russia
81.	Meiji	1852-1912	Japan
82.	Tilak	1856-1920	India
83.	Reontgen	1845-1923	Germany
84.	Lenin	1870-1924	Russia
85.	Sun Yat-sen	1866-1925	China
86.	Marie Curie	1867-1934	Poland & France
87.	Rudyard Kipling	1865-1936	Great Britain
88.	Jagdis Chandra Bose	1858-1937	India
89.	Marconi	1874-1937	Italy
90.	Rabindranath Tagore	1861-1941	India
91.	Romain Rolland	1866-1944	France
92.	Aurobindo	1872-1950	India
93.	Franklin D. Roosevelt	1882-1945	USA
94.	Wright brothers	1867-1912 1871-1948	USA
95.	Gandhi	1869-1948	India
96.	Montessori	1870-1952	Italy
97.	Einstein	1879-1955	Germany & USA
98.	Neils Bohr	1885-1962	Denmark
99.	Winston Churchill	1874-1965	Great Britain
100.	Albert Schweitzer	1875-1965	France & Gabon
101.	Martin Luther King,Jr.	1929-1968	USA

102.	C. V. Raman	1888-1970	India
103.	Field Marshal Slim	1891-1970	Great Britain
104.	Mao Tse-tung	1893-1976	China
105.	Heisenberg	1901-1976	Germany
106.	Mother Teresa	1910-	Former Yugoslavia & India
107.	Har Gobind Khorana	1922-	India & USA
108.	Satya Sai Baba	1926-	India

Note

Many more names can be added to this list. To read books about the lives of the individuals in the list, please consult:

* *Encyclopaedia Britannica.*

* *One Hundred Great Modern Lives,* edited by John Canning, Century Books, 1975.

* *The One Hundred—A Ranking of the Most Influential Persons in History,* by Michael Hart, rev. ed, Carol Publishing Group, 1992.

Notes

Chapter 1

1. *Mahabharata,* trans. K. Subhramaniam (Bombay: Bharathi Vidya Bhavan); Jack Hawley, *Reawakening the Spirit in Work: The Power of Dharmic Management* (San Francisco: Berrett-Koehler, 1993).
2. Lt. Gen. (ret.) Dr. M. L. Chibber and others, *Strategy and Leadership,* Textbook MS 91, rev. ed. (New Delhi: School of Management, Indira Gandhi National Open University, 1992).
3. Ibid.
4. Stephen R. Covey, *The Seven Habits of Highly Effective People* (New York: Simon and Schuster, 1990).
5. Sathya Sai Baba, quoted in Seema Kundra, *Facets of the Divine Diamond* (Prasanthi Nilayam, India: Sri Sathya Sai Books and Publications Trust).

Chapter 2

1. Lord Moran, *Anatomy of Courage* (London; reprint, Dehra Dun, India: Book World, 1984).
2. Covey, *Habits of Highly Effective People.*
3. Sathya Sai Baba, discussion on leadership, with M.B.A. students and teachers, Sri Sathya Sai Institute of Higher Learning, Prasanthi Nilayam, India.
4. An Experienced Executive, leadership seminar for executive class, M.B.A. program, Pepperdine University, July 1992.
5. Sai Baba, discussion on leadership.
6. Sathya Sai Baba.
7. John Adair, *Action Centered Leadership* (London: McGraw-Hill, 1973).

Chapter 3

1. Adair, *Action Centered Leadership.*
2. Marshall Sashkin, "A New Vision of Leadership," *Journal of Management Development* 6.4 (1989).
3. Taya Zinkin, magazine article, *Opinion* (3 November 1981).
4. John Adair, *Effective Leadership: A Self-Development Manual* (Aldershot, England: Gower, 1983).
5. Ibid.
6. Covey, *Habits of Highly Effective People.*
7. Sai Baba, discussion on leadership.

8. Swami Vivekananda, quoted in Narayan Vaghul, Raja Ramdeo Anandilal Podar Sixteenth Memorial Lecture, Jaipur, India, 10 December 1988.
9. Field Marshal Von Moltke, quoted in Sir Ian Hamilton, *Soul and Body of an Army* (London: E. Arnold, 1921).
10. Viktor E. Frankl, *Man's Search for Meaning*, Signet Paperback.
11. John Heider, *Tao of Leadership: Lao Tzu's Tao te Ching Adapted for a New Age* (Aldershot, England: Hante Wildwood House, 1985).
12. Francis Bacon, *The Essays or Counsels, Civill and Morall* (London: Hamn and Barret, 1625).
13. Ibid.
14. Lt. Gen. (ret.) Dr. M. L. Chibber, *How to Be a Successful Leader*, 3rd ed. (New Delhi: ANA, 1985).
15. Ibid.
16. Hawley, *Dharmic Management*.
17-20. Ibid.

Chapter 4

1. S. L. A. Marshal, *Officer as a Leader* (Harrizburg: Telegraph Press).
2. Peter F. Drucker, *The Effective Executive* (William Heinemann, 1982).
3. Sathya Sai Baba, discourse on spirituality, Kodaikanal, India, 7 April 1993.
4. Sathya Sai Baba, *Sathya Sai Speaks,* vols. 1-11, comp. N. Kasturi (Prasanthi Nilayam, India: Sri Sathya Sai Books and Publications Trust, 1974-1985).
5. Field Marshal Sir William Slim, *Courage and Other Broadcasts* (London: Cassel, 1957).
6. Sai Baba, discussion on leadership.
7. Drucker, *Effective Executive*.

Chapter 5

1. Lidell I. Hart, *Strategy of Indirect Approach* (London: Faber and Faber).
2. Field Marshal Sir John Hacket, *The Profession of Arms* (London: Sidgwick & Jackson, 1983).
3. Chibber, *Successful Leader*.
4. Covey, *Habits of Highly Effective People*.
5. Adair, *Effective Leadership*.
6. Anthony D'Souza, *Leadership: A Trilogy on Leadership and Management* (Bombay: BYB Haggai Institute).

Chapter 6

1. Robert L. Katz, "Skill of an Effective Administrator," *Harvard Business Review* (January-February 1955): 33-42.
2. Adair, *Effective Leadership.*
3. Paul M. Kennedy, *Preparing for the Twenty-First Century* (1992).
4. Sathya Sai Baba, discourse, Kodaikanal, India, April 1993.
5. Ibid.
6. Jawaharlal Nehru, *Discovery of India.*

Chapter 7

1. Sathya Sai Baba, speaking at university convocation (an ancient Indian spiritual experience going back thousands of years), Sri Sathya Sai Institute of Higher Learning, 22 November 1990.
2. Zinkin, magazine article.
3. Edwin G. Boring, *Psychology of Armed Services* (USA: Harvard University; Dehra Dun, India: Natraj, 1973).
4. Dr. Sivananda, *Self Knowledge* (Sivananda Nagar, India: Divine Life Society P. O.)
5. Peter F. Drucker, *The Effective Executive* (London: Pan Books).
6-8. Ibid.
9. Covey, *Habits of Highly Effective People.*
10.Ibid.
11.Ibid.
12.Aldous Huxley, *The Perennial Philosophy* (Harper and Row, 1970).
13.Sai Baba, *Sathya Sai Speaks*, vol 4.
14.Huxley, *Perennial Philosophy.*
15.Ibid.
16.Ibid.

Chapter 8

1. Covey, *Habits of Highly Effective People.*
2. Ibid.
3. Ibid.
4. Ram Tirath, quoted in Dr. Safaya, *Great Educators of India* (Ambala).
5. Sathya Sai Baba, address to students, Sathya Sai High School, India, December 1990.
6. Swami Vivekananda, "Powers of the Mind," address in Los Angeles on 8 January 1900, in *The Complete Works of Swami Vivekananda,* vol 2 (Ramakrishna Mission).

7. Covey, *Habits of Highly Effective People.*
8. Sathya Sai Baba, quoted in Peggy Mason and Ron Laing, *Sathya Sai Baba: The Embodiment of Love* (London: Sawbridge, 1982).
9. Sathya Sai Baba, quoted in *Sai Avatar* (Calcutta: C. J. Gandhi Welfare Trust, 1975).
10. Sathya Sai Baba, quoted in Kundra, *Divine Diamond.*
11. Sathya Sai Baba, quoted in *Words of Jesus and Sathya Sai Baba,* comp. Dr. H. K. Takyi and Kishin J. Khubchandani (Accra, Ghana).
12. Dr. Hans Salye, quoted in Covey, *Habits of Highly Effective People.*
13. Ibid.
14. Ibid.
15. John Canning, *One Hundred Great Modern Lives* (London: Century Books, 1975).
16. Benjamin Franklin, *Autobiography* (Boston: Houghton-Mifflin, 1923).
17-33. Ibid.
34. Canning, *Great Modern Lives.*
35. Louis Fischer, *The Life of Mahatma Gandhi* (London: Jonathan Cape, 1951).
36-40. Ibid.
41. M. K. Gandhi, *An Autobiography: Or the Story of My Experiments with Truth,* 10th ed. (Ahmedabad, India: Navjivan).
42. Sathya Sai Baba, lecture at *Summer Course 1993,* 26 May 1993.
43. Fischer, *Life of Mahatma Gandhi.*
44-49. Ibid.
50. Henry Thomas and Diana Lee Thomas, *Living Biographies of Religious Leaders* (Bharatiya Vidya Bhavan).
51. Fischer, *Life of Mahatma Gandhi.*
52. Thomas and Thomas, *Living Biographies.*
53. Rajendra Prasad, President of India, quoted in *Collected Works of Mahatama Gandhi,* vol 1 (India: Publications Division, Government of India, 1958).
54. Ibid.
55. Fischer, *Life of Mahatma Gandhi.*
56. Ibid.
57. Justice R. S. Sarkaria, "Media's Battle against Fundamentalism," address in Bangalore, India, *Hindu,* 12 June 1993.
58. Fischer, *Life of Mahatma Gandhi.*
59. Ibid.
60. Prasad, quoted in *Collected Works of Mahatma Gandhi.*
61. Winston S. Churchill, *My Early Life; A Roving Commission,* school ed. (9th reprint: Odham Press, 1960).
62-71. Ibid.

72.Winston S. Churchill, A *History of the English-Speaking Peoples* (New York: Dodd, Mead, 1961).
73.Churchill, *My Early Life*.

Chapter 9

1. Swami Vivekananda, quoted in Safaya, *Great Educators of India*.
2. Ibid.
3. Sai Baba, *Sathya Sai Speaks*.
4. Ibid.
5. Zinkin, magazine article.
6. Sai Baba, lecture at *Summer Course 1993*.
7. Sai Baba, *Sathya Sai Speaks*.
8. Ibid.
9. Arnold Toynbee, *Choose Life*, a dialogue between Toynbee and Daisaku Ikeda (Delhi: Oxford University Press, 1987).
10.Benoy Ghosh, *Ishwar Chandra Vidyasagar,* Builders of Modern India Series (India: Government of India).
11.Ibid.
12.Vaghul, Raja Ramdeo Anandilal Podar Sixteenth Memorial Lecture.
13.Swami Dayananda Saraswati, *Satyartha Prakash*.
14.Sathya Sai Baba, address to university teachers, 1991.
15.Phillip Mason, *The Matter of Honour* (Penguin Books, 1974).
16.Toynbee, *Choose Life*.
17.Sathya Sai Baba, *Vidya Vahini* (Prasanthi Nilayam, India: Sri Sathya Sai Books and Publications Trust, 1984).
18.Tirath, quoted in Safaya, *Great Educators of India*.
19.Toynbee, *Choose Life*.
20.Vivekananda, quoted in Safaya, *Great Educators of India*.
21.Ibid.
22.Sathya Sai Baba.
23.Churchill, *My Early Life*.
24.Swami Dayananda Saraswati, quoted in Safaya, *Great Educators of India*.
25.Toynbee, *Choose Life*.

References

Chapter I

1. K. Subhramaniam, *Mahabhartha*, Bharathi Vidya Bhavan, Bombay and Jack Hawleys *Power of Dharmic Management*, Beffet-Kochler, San Francisco 1993
2. Lt. Gen. (Dr.) M. L. Chibber and others *Strategy and Leadership*, Indira Gandhi National Open University textbook MS 91
3. Ibid
4. Covey Stephen R., *7 Habits of Highly Effective People*, Simon and Shuster, New York, 1990
5. Sai Baba in *Facets of Divine Diamonds*.

Chapter 2

1. Lord Moran, *Anatomy of courage*, Book World, Dehra Dun 1984.
2. Stephen R Covey, *Habits of Highly Effective People*, Simon and Schuster, New York 1990.
3. *Mahavakya* is the term used for the short and crisp eternal truths articulated in the most ancient literature of humanity-Vedas. Aldous Huxley, using one of them *thou art that* as the theme, wrote his seminal book the *Perennial Philosophy*.
4. Sai Baba while discussing leadership with the students and teachers of MBA class at the Sai university.
5. Expression by an experienced executive in a leadership seminar at the Pepperdine University for the Executive MBA class held in July 1992.
6. Sai Baba while discussing Leadership.
7. Sai Baba.
8. Adair, John in *Action Centered Leadership*, McGraw Hill: London 1973.

Chapter 3

1. Adair John in *Action Centered Leadership*, Mc Graw Hill, London, 1973.
2. Marshall Sashkin, *A New Vision of Leadership*, National Institute of Education Washington DC in Journal of Management Development 6.4 of 1989.
3. Taya Zinkin in magazine *Opinion*-New Delhi of November 3,1981.
4. Adair John in *Effective Leadership*, Gower Publishing Company, Aldershot, England 1983.
5. Ibid.

6. Covey Stephen R in *The 7 Habits of Highly Effective People*, Simon and Schuster, New York 1990.
7. Chancellor Sai university, during interaction with MBA students on leadership.
8. Swami Vivekananda quoted by N Vaghulin *Raja Ramdeo Anandilal Podar Sixteenth Memorial Lecture*, at Jaipur, India, on December 10, 1988.
9. Quoted by Sir Ian Hamilton in *Soul and Body of our Army*, E.Amold and Company, London 1921.
10. Frankl Victor in *Man's Search For Meaning*, Signet paper back.
11. Heider John in *Tao of Leadership*, Hante Wildwood House, Adershot, England, 1985.
12. Francis Bacon in *The Essays-Civil and Moral*, Ambition, Hamn Barret, 1625.
13. Ibid.
14. Chibber Dr M. L. Lieut General, in *How to be a Successful Leader*, third edition, ANA Publishing House, New Delhi 1985.
15. Ibid.
16. Hawley Jack-in *The Power of Dharmic Management*, Berrett-Kochler Publishers-San Francisco, 1993.
17. Ibid.
18. Ibid.
19. Ibid.
20. Ibid.

Chapter 4

I. Marshal SLA-in *Officer as a Leader*, Telegraph Press Harrizburg
2. Drucker Peter-in *The Effective Executive*, William Heinemann Ltd., 1982
3. Satya Sai Baba-in discourse on *spirituality* at KODAIKANAL (India), on 7 April, 1993
4. Satya Sai Baba in *Satya Sai Speaks*.
5. Slim, Sir William, Field Marshal in *Courage and other Broadcasts*, Cassel and Company, London, 1957.
6. Satya Sai Baba during interaction with MBA students on *Leadership*.
7. Drucker Peter in *The Effective Executive*.

Chapter 5

1. Hart Lidel I., in *Strategy of Indirect Approach*, Fabre and Fabre Ltd., London.
2. Hacket, Sir John, Field Marshal, in *Profession of Arms*, Sidwick & Jackson, London 1983.

3. Chibber (Dr.) M. L. Lt. Gen in *How to be a Successful Leader*, third edition ANA Publishing House, New Delhi 1986.
4. Covey Stephen R., in *The 7 Habits of Highly Effective People*.
5. Adair John in *Effective Leadership*.
6. D'Souza Anthony in *Leadership*, BYB Haggai Institute, Bandra, Bombay.

Chapter 6

1. Katz Robert L., in *Skill of an Effective Administrator*, Harvard Business Review, p33-42, Jan-Feb 1955.
2. Adair John in *Effective Leadership*, Gower, Aldershot England 1983.
3. Kennedy Paul in *Preparing for 21st Century*, 1992.
4. Sai Baba in discourses at Kodaikanal, India, April 1993.
5. Ibid.
6. Nehru, Jawaharlal in *Discovery of India*.

Chapter 7

1. Chancellor Sri saya Sai university, speaking at the Convocation of the University, 22 November 1990. This is an ancient spiritual experience in India going back thousands of years.
2. Zinkin Taya in *Opinion*, New Delhi, 3 December 1981.
3. Boring Edwin C. in *Psychology of Armed Services*. Harvard University; Printed in India by Natraj Publishers, Dehra Dun 1973.
4. Dr. Sivananda in *Self Knowledge*, Divine Life Society P. O., Sivananda Nagar (UP).
5. Drucker Peter F. in *Effective Executive*, Pan Books London.
6. Ibid.
7. Ibid.
8. Ibid.
9. Covey Stephen Rin *The 7 habits of Highly Effective People*, Simon and Schuster, New York, 1990.
10. Ibid.
11. Ibid. (quoted)
12. Huxley Aldous in *The Perennial Philosophy*, Harper and Row, Publishers-1970.
13. Satya Sai Baba in *Satya Sai Speaks*, Vol 4, Shri Satya Sai Books and Publication Trust, Prasanthi Nilayam (AP) 515131.
14. Huxley Aldous.
15. Ibid.
16. Ibid.

Chapter 8

1. Stephen R Covey in *The 7 Habits of Highly Effective People.*
2. Ibid.
3. Ibid.
4. Ram Tirath quoted in *Great Educators of India*, by Dr. Safaya, Ambala.
5. Satya Sai Baba's address to students of Satya Sai High School, Dec 1990.
6. Vivekananda in his address at Los Angeles on *Powers of the mind*, 8 Jan 1900. See collected works of *Vivekananda Vol II*, Ramakrishna Mission Publication.
7. Stephen Covey.
8. Satya Sai Baba quoted by Peggy Mason and Ron Laing in *Embodiment of Love*, Sawbridge Enterprise, London.
9. Satya Sai Baba, in *Sai Avatar Sayings*, by C. J. Gandhi Welfare Trust Calcutta, 1975.
10. Satya Sai Baba in *Facets of the Divine Diamonds*, Sri saya Sai Publication Trust.
11. Satya Sai Baba in *Words of Jesus and Satya Sai Baba*, compiled by Dr HK Raky, FRCS, Accra, Ghana.
12. Quoted by Stephen Covey.
13. Ibid.
14. Ibid.
16. John Canning in *l00 Great Lives*, Century Books Ltd, London 1975.
17. Benjamin Franklin in *Autobiography*, Hovgton Mifflin, Boston 1923.
18.
to
34. Ibid.
35. John Canning.
36. Louis Fischer, in *The Life of Mahatma Gandhi*, Jonathan Cape, London, 1951.
37
to
41. Ibid.
42. M. K. Gandhi in *My Experiments with Truth*, Navjivan Publishing House Ahmedabad, India(10th edition).
43. Satya Sai Baba, in Lecture on 26 May to students of Summer Course 1993.
44. Louis Fischer.
45
to
50. Ibid.

51. Henry Thomas and Diana Lee Thomas, in *Living Biographies of Religious Leaders*, Bharatiya Vidya Bhavan.
52. Louis Fischer.
53. Henry Thomas and Diana Lee Thomas.
54. Rajendra Prasad, President of India, in collected works of *Mahatama Gandhi Vol 1*, Publications Division, Government of India 1958 55. Ibid.
56. Louis Fischer.
57. Ibid.
58. Justice R. S. Sarkaria in address on *Media's Battle Against Fundamentalism* at Bangalore, published in *Hindu* of 12 June 1993.
59. Louis Fischer.
60. Ibid.
61. Rajendra Prasad.
62. Winston Churchill in *My Early Life*, School Edition, Odham Press, 9th reprint, 1960.
63.
to
72. Ibid.
73. Winston Churchill,in *The History of the English Speaking People*, Dodd, Mead and Company, New York 1961.
74. Winston Churchill, *My Early Life*.

Chapter 9

1. Vivekananda quoted by D. Safaya in *Great Educators of India*, Ambala Publishers.
2. Ibid.
3. Satya Sai Baba in *Satya Sai Speaks*, Satya Sai Book and Publication Trust, Prasanthi Nilayam.
4. Ibid.
5. Taya Zinkin.
6. Satya Sai Baba in lecture to *Summer Course 1993*-26 May 1993.
7. Satya Sai Baba in *Satya Sai Speaks*.
8. Ibid.
8a. Ibid.
9. Toynbee Arnold and Ikeda Daisoku in *Chose Life*, Oxford University Press, Delhi, 1987.
10. Benoy Ghosh in *Ishwar Chandra Vidyasagar* in the series,-Builders of Modern India, Government of India Publication.
11. Ibid.
12. Vaghul Narayan in Raja Ramdeo Anandilal Podar sixteenth memorial lecture on 10 December 1988 at Jaipur (India).
13. Dayananda in *sayarath Prakash*.

14. Satya Sai Baba in an address to the University teachers 1991.
15. Mason Phillip in *The Matter of Honor*, Penguin Books, 1974.
16. Toynbee and Ikeda.
17. Satya Sai Baba in *Vidya Vahini*, Satya Sai Book and Publication trust.
18. See chapter-6 on dealing with people.
19. Ram Tirath quoted in *Great Educators of India*.
20. Toynbee and Ikeda.
21. Vivekananda quoted in *Great Educators of India*.
22. Ibid.
23. Satya Sai Baba.
24. Winston Churchill in *My Early Life*.
25. Dayananda quoted in *Great Educators of India*.
26. Toynbee and Ikeda.

Bibliography

Adair, John. *Action Centered Leadership.* London: McGraw-Hill, 1973..

_____.*Effective Leadership: A Self-Development Manual.* Aldershot, England: Gower, 1983.

_____.*Skills of Leadership.* Aldershot, England: Gower, 1984.

Bacon, Francis. *The Essayes or Counsels, Civill and Morall.* London: Hamn and Barret, 1625.

Bennis, Warren, and Burt Nanus. *Leaders: The Strategies for Taking Charge.* Cambridge: Harper and Row, 1985.

Blake, Robert R., and Jane S. Mouton. *Executive Achievement: Making It at the Top.* New York: McGraw-Hill, 1986.

Blake, Robert B., and Others. *Spectacular Teamwork____How to Develop the Leadership Skills for Team Success.* London: Sidgwick and Jackson, 1987.

Boring, Edwin G. *Psychology for Armed Services.* USA: Harvard University. Reprint, Dehra Dun, India: Natraj, 1973.

Brown and Cohn. *The Study of Leadership.* Dep Interstate: Danvill, 1958.

Burns, James MacGregor. *Leadership.* Harvard Ed. Reprint, New Delhi: Ambika, 1978.

Canning, John. *One Hundred Great Modern Lives.* London: Century Books, 1975.

Chibber, Lt. Gen. (ret.) Dr. M. L. *Military Leadership to Prevent Military Coup.* New Delhi: Lancer International, 1986.

_____.*How to Be a Successful Leader.* 3rd ed. New Delhi: ANA, 1985.

Chibber, Lt. Gen. (ret.) Dr. M. L., and Others. *Strategy and Leadership.* Textbook MS 91. Rev. ed. New Delhi: School of Management, Indira Gandhi National Open University, 1992.

Chinmayananda, Swami. *The Art of Manmaking.* Madras, India: Chinmaya Publication Trust.

Churchill, Winston. S. *My Early Life; A Roving Commission.* School ed. 9th reprint, Odham Press, 1960.

      .*A History of the English-Speaking Peoples.* New York: Dodd, Mead, 1961.

Collected Works of Mahatma Gandhi. Vol 1. India: Publications Division, Government of India, 1958.

Covey, Stephen R. *The Seven Habits of Highly Effective People.* New York: Simon and Schuster, 1990.

Drucker, Peter F. *The Effective Executive.* William Heinemann, 1982.

D'Souza, Anthony. *Leadership: A Trilogy on Leadership and Management.* Bombay: BYB Haggai Institute.

Fischer, Louis. *The Life of Mahatma Gandhi.* London: Jonathan Cape, 1951.

Franklin, Benjamin. *Autobiography.* Boston: Houghton-Mifflin, 1923.

Frankl, Viktor E. *Man's Search for Meaning.* Signet Paperback.

Gandhi, M. K. *An Autobiography: Or the Story of My Experiments with Truth.* 10th ed. Ahmedabad, India: Navjivan.

Ghosh, Benoy. *Ishwar Chandra Vidyasagar.* Builders of Modern India Series. India: Government of India.

Gibb, C. A. *Leadership___Selected Reading.* Middlesex: Harmondworth, Penguin Books, 1969.

Hackett, Sir John Field Marshall. *The Profession of Arms.* London: Sidgwick and Jackson, 1983.

Hamilton, Ian. *The Soul and Body of an Army.* London: E. Arnold, 1921.

Hart, Lidell I. *Strategy of Indirect Approach.* London: Faber and Faber.

Hart, Michael H. *The One Hundred: A Ranking of the Most Influential Persons in History USA.* Reprint, Madras, India: Meera, 1991

Hawley, Jack. *Reawakening the Spirit in Work: The Power of Dharmic Management.* San Francisco: Berrett-Koehler, 1993.

Heider, John. *Tao of Leadership: Lao Tzu's Tao te Ching Adapted for a New Age.* Aldershot, England: Hante Wildwood House, 1985.

Hickman, Craig R., and Michael A. Silva. *The Future 500___Creating Tomorrow's Organizations Today.* New York: NAL Books, 1987.

Huxley, Aldous. *The Perennial Philosophy.* Harper and Row, 1970.

Kasturi, N. *Sathyam Sivam Sundaram.* 4 vols. Prasanthi Nilayam, India: Sri Sathya Sai Books and Publications Trust. The life story of Sathya Sai Baba.

Katz, Robert L. "Skill of an Effective Administrator." *Harvard Business Review* (January-February 1955): 33-42.

Kennedy, Paul M. *Preparing for the Twenty-First Century.* 1992.

Kundra, Seema. *Facets of the Divine Diamond.* Prasanthi Nilayam, India: Sri Sathya Sai Books and Publications Trust.

Lal, R. M. *In Search of Leadership.* New Delhi: Vision Books, 1986.

Marshall, S. L. A. *Officer as a Leader.* Harrizburg: Telegraph Press.

Mason, Peggy, and Ron Laing. *Sathya Sai Baba: The Embodiment of Love.* London: Sawbridge, 1982.

Mason, Phillip. *The Matter of Honour.* Penguin Books, 1974.

McCormack, Mark H. *What They Don't Teach You at Harvard Business School: Notes from a Street-Smart Executive.* Fontana Cullina, 1985.

Moran, Lord. *Anatomy of Courage.* London. Reprint, Dehra Dun, India: Book World, 1984.

Nehru, Jawaharlal. *Discovery of India.*

Peale, Norman Vincent, and Kenneth H. Blanchard. *Power of Ethical Management.* New York: William Morrow, 1988.

Safaya, Dr. *Great Educators of India.* Ambala.

Sai Avatar. Calcutta: C. J. Gandhi Welfare Trust, 1975.

Sai Baba, Sathya. *Sathya Sai Speaks.* Vols 1-11. Comp. N. Kasturi. Prasanthi Nilayam, India: Sri Sathya Sai Books and Publications Trust, 1974-1985.

_____.*Vidya Vahini.* Prasanthi Nilayam, India: Sri Sathya Sai Books and Publications Trust, 1984.

Saraswati, Swami Dayananda. *Satyartha Prakash.*

Sashkin, Marshall. "A New Vision of Leadership." *Journal of Management Development* 6.4 (1989).

Sayles, Leonard R. *Leadership: What Effective Managers Really Do and How They Do It.* New York: McGraw-Hill, 1979.

Sivananda, Dr. *Self Knowledge.* Sivananda Nagar, India: Divine Life Society P. O.

Slim, Sir William Field Marshal. *Defeat into Victory.* London: Cassel.

_____.*Courage and Other Broadcasts.* London: Cassel, 1957.

Subhramaniam, K., trans. *Mahabharata.* Bombay: Bharathi Vidya Bhavan.

Takyi, Dr. H. K., and Kishin J. Khubchandani, comps. *Words of Jesus and Sathya Sai Baba.* Accra, Ghana.

Thomas, Henry, and Diana Lee Thomas. *Living Biographies of Religious Leaders.* Bharatiya Vidya Bhavan.

Toynbee, Arnold. *Choose Life.* A dialogue between Toynbee and Daisaku Ikeda. Delhi: Oxford University Press, 1987.

Vivekananda, Swami. "Powers of the Mind." An address in Los Angeles on 8 January 1900. In *The Complete Works of Swami Vivekananda.* Vol 2. Ramakrishna Mission.

AUTHOR

Lieutenant General Dr. M. L. Chibber, Retired

Born in August 1927, the author hails from the Northwest Frontier Province of India. His 40-year career in the Army culminated in his being commander in chief of India's Northern Command, which was comprised of about 300,000 personnel deployed in eyeball-to-eyeball contact in a "no peace, no war" confrontation with China and Pakistan. During that confrontation, he masterminded the operation to protect the Siachen Glacier from being captured by Pakistan.

An officer of the Fifth Gorkha Rifles, Lt. Gen. Chibber held important appointments like the commander of India's counteroffensive force, adjutant general, and director of military operations. He was on the faculty of the Indian Military Academy and the Defence Services Staff College, India. In 1953, he served in Korea on the first UN peace mission. During his illustrious military career, Lt. Gen. Chibber also pioneered the establishment of the Army Institute of National Integration and consolidated the Army Group Insurance and Army Welfare Housing Organization. He retired from the army in August 1985.

After retirement, he became defence adviser to the Fourth Pay Commission. Thereafter, for four years (1986-89), he served as chief executive of the Management Development Institute, New Delhi, where he continues as visiting professor. He also serves on the Board of Studies for M.B.A. and is a member of the Academic Council.of the Sri Sathya Sai Institute of Higher Learning (deemed university).

A graduate of the British Army Staff College, Lt. Gen. Chibber has a M.Sc. from Madras University and a Ph.D. from Allahabad University. Other academic honors include: Fellow of the Interuniversity Seminar on Armed Forces and Society, Chicago; from 1990 to 1991, Jawaharlal Nehru Fellow researching the introduction of national service in India; and Fellow of Arms Control, Disarmament and International Security, University of Illinois, Urbana. Lt. Gen. Chibber has authored many books and

211

numerous monographs and articles on leadership and matters related to security, war and peace.

He is active in India and abroad in teaching, research and development in areas of leadership, introduction of national service in India, and India-Pakistan reconciliation, etc.

Lt. Gen. Chibber was awarded the Ati Vishisht Seva Medal, a Medal for Highly Distinguished Service in 1972, and the Param Vishisht Seva Medal, a Medal for Highest Distinguished Service in 1976. In 1986, the National Honour of Padma Bhushan Lotus Decoration was conferred on him for exceptional service to the nation.

Books

1. *Military Leadership to Prevent Military Coup*, based on Ph.D. thesis, Lancer International, New Delhi, 1986.
2. *Soldiers Role in National Integration,* Lancer International, New Delhi, 1986.
3. *How to Be a Successful Leader,* third edition, ANA Publishers, New Delhi, 1986.
4. Coauthor, *Strategy and Leadership,* second edition, textbook for M.B.A. program, Indira Gandhi National Open University, New Delhi, 1992.
5. *History of Jammu and Kashmir Light Infantry*, JAK LI Regimental Center, Srinagar, 1992.
6. Chapter on "The Quest for Security," in *Indian Foreign Policy—The Indira Gandhi Years*, Radiant, New Delhi, 1990.
7. Chapter on "India-Pakistan Reconciliation," in *South Asia after the Cold War: International Perspectives*, Westview, USA, 1993.
8. *National Service for Defence, Development and National Integration of India*, Kartikeya Publications, New Delhi, 1995.